DURBAN DIALOGUES DISSECTED

An Analysis of Ashwin Singh's Plays

Edited by Felicity Hand

SUN PRESS

Durban Dialogues Dissected: An Analysis of Ashwin Singh's Plays

Published by African Sun Media under the SUN PReSS imprint

This publication was subjected to an independent double-blind peer evaluation by the publisher.

The editor and the publisher have made every effort to obtain permission for and acknowledge the use of copyrighted material. Refer all enquiries to the publisher.

Views reflected in this publication are not necessarily those of the publisher.

First edition 2020

ISBN 978-1-928357-64-3
ISBN 978-1-928357-65-0 (e-book)
https://doi.org/10.18820/9781928357650

Set in Baskerville 10/13

Cover design, typesetting and production by African Sun Media

SUN PReSS is an imprint of African Sun Media. Scholarly, professional and reference works are published under this imprint in print and electronic formats.

This publication can be ordered from:
orders@africansunmedia.co.za
Takealot: bit.ly/2monsfl
Google Books: bit.ly/2k1Uilm
africansunmedia.store.it.si *(e-books)*
Amazon Kindle: amzn.to/2ktL.pkL

Visit africansunmedia.co.za for more information.

Contents

SCENE 6

ACT 3
SCENE 1

SCENE 2

List of Abbreviations

The following abbreviations are used throughout the text for quotations from Ashwin Singh's plays.

H   *To House*

SS   *Spice 'n' Stuff*

Sh   *Shooting*

RL   *Reoca Light*

D   *Duped*

BBB   *Beyond the Big Bangs*

Sw   *Swing*

IG   *Into the Grey*

Note on Terminology

We have chosen not to unify the authors' use of the term *black* so readers are encouraged to think beyond straightforward definitions. Each author uses the term in his or her own way and spells it with either a capital B or a small letter b. Likewise, authors have opted for capital or lower case letters for other ethnicities, such as white or coloured, in accordance with their specific purpose.

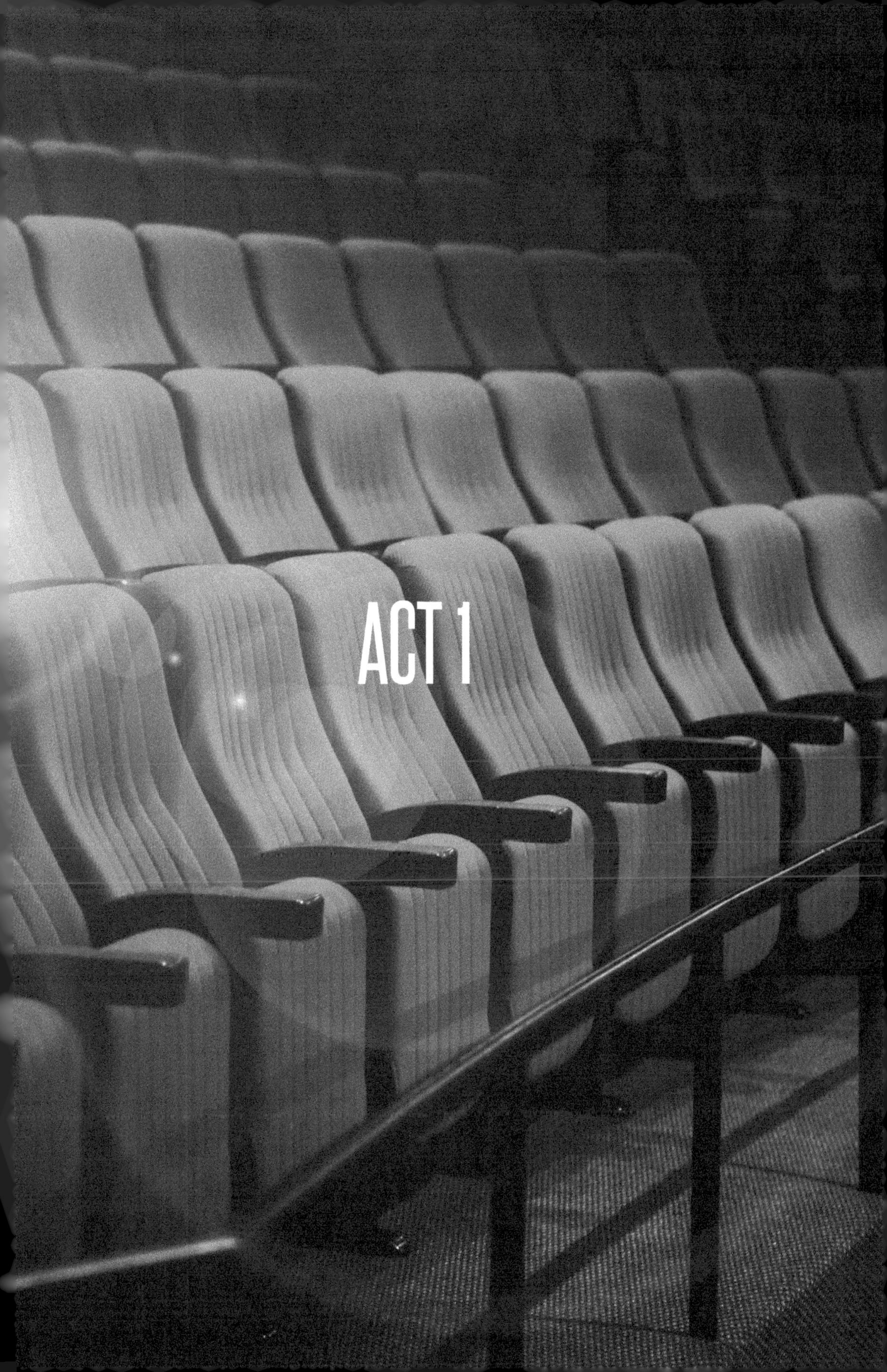

ACT 1

SCENE 1

Ashwin Singh's Drama: Reconstructing South Africanness

Felicity Hand

I first made Ashwin Singh's acquaintance via email over three years ago in 2017 and since then we have met on two occasions in Durban and have kept up a regular email correspondence together with Skype conversations. Ashwin contacted me as he had heard about a forthcoming publication I had co-edited with Esther Pujolràs-Noguer which contained a chapter on his play *To House* written by Coplen Rose, who has also contributed to this volume. To my shame, I was not very familiar with South African drama at all as I had tended to specialize in novels and short stories with some occasional poetry. However, over the last three years I have realized how much I had been missing and I have since incorporated several South African plays, including of course Ashwin's, into my syllabus. A highlight of one of my trips to Durban was watching a brilliant performance of Ashwin's 2017 play *Into the Grey*, in which he acted. I was deeply honoured to be invited to edit this volume of essays on Ashwin Singh's work and it is no exaggeration to say that the experience of working with Ashwin himself and the interaction with the authors in this volume has enriched me enormously.

~

In 1980s South Africa collective community theatre was identified with the soul of resistance to the oppressive apartheid state. Theatre traditions in the country were centred around the Struggle as the Black Consciousness Movement had inspired much political theatre from the 1970s onwards. Art clearly has a crucial role to play in disseminating political ideas, especially in dictatorial regimes, and to mention just one well known example, Maishe Maponya's *The Hungry Earth* (1979) called for resistance to the repressive apartheid state (Gilbert, 2007). The individual protester was obliged to find his or her niche within this community and by not conforming to the collective voice, he or she would have run the risk of being, at best, misunderstood and, at worst, categorized as indifferent or even hostile to the Struggle (Nuttall & Michael, 2000: 10-11). By the 1990s, when the demise of apartheid was becoming a reality, more strident individual voices were beginning to be heard. Director Mark Fleishman notes how new identities were gradually being forged, which would slowly dismantle rigid categories implemented by apartheid philosophy (Nuttall & Michael, 2000: 209). Despite the move towards an inclusive nation-building project, old racial fixations and stereotypes die hard. The first two decades of a democratic South Africa may have rendered protest theatre somewhat obsolete but a firm belief in a creolized community, where the sharing of a common space leads to an intermingling of cultures, languages and customs without any hierarchical ranking, still seems to be in the making (Nuttall & Michael, 2000: 6-7). As regards specific Indian South African theatre, according to Neilish Bose (2009: 366), the Struggle did not enter into local drama until the 1960s when issues of discrimination and unfair apartheid laws began to feature in plays. Thomas Blom Hansen (2000: 256) notes that Durban Indians began to foment their own tradition of drama, satirical plays and outright political commentary from this time but even today they are still enmeshed in a crisis of representation, which manifests itself in the wider South African arena.

The plays of Ronnie Govender, who "inaugurated the genre of Indian South African theatre" (Rastogi, 2008: 222), focussed exclusively on the Indian South African community, which, being mainly quite conservative in outlook, shied away from excessive radicalism in its attempt to obtain middle-class respectability, making it, in the words of the playwright, "its own worst enemy" (ibid:232). These early Indian South African plays, including those by Kessie Govender, Kriben Pillay as well as Ronnie Govender's own work, sought to delve into the complexity of the Indian community, so often reduced to what Hansen describes as the "older 'coolie' stereotypes [with their] funny accents, superstition, snobbery and patriarchal control of women" (Hansen, 2000: 267-268). These plays, with their "internalist character [of] self-mockery of vices and accents" (ibid: 258) highlight the internal racism and classism of the community while also attempting to celebrate the "new interracial solidarities and levels of understanding between non-whites" (ibid). In this respect Kessie Govender's *Working Class Hero* needs to be singled out for its brave denunciation of Indian racism towards Black Africans.[1] Following on from Nuttall & Michael's claim that twenty-first century South Africanness should be conceived in terms of a creolized identity, I claim that the plays of Ashwin Singh celebrate this creolization as his characters strive to come to terms with the post-apartheid situation which acknowledges – or should acknowledge – the contribution of cultures from the other ethnic groups in the "new" South Africa. In fact, Ronnie Govender laments what he calls the lost possibility of a common South African identity, free from apartheid categories (Rastogi, 2008: 223), which is a theme that resurfaces in post-apartheid drama, including Ashwin Singh's work.

This volume aims to insert Ashwin Singh's oeuvre into the postcolonial canon of drama but before I proceed to justify this well-deserved position, I wish to make a few comments on the absence of drama in far too much postcolonial criticism

---

1   In this respect Ashwin Desai and Goolam Vahed's somewhat controversial 2016 publication suggests that Gandhi showed little sympathy towards the Africans. They argue that he collaborated to their subjugation and perpetuated racist stereotypes about black people by insisting on the Aryan connection between Indians and Europeans.

and – I lament to add – in far too many university postcolonial syllabi. In *Post-Colonial Drama*, Gilbert and Tompkins note that "most post-colonial criticism overlooks drama, perhaps because of its apparently impure form: playscripts are only a part of a theatre experience, and performance is therefore difficult to document" (1996: 8). This is undoubtedly true as many of the plays of the Black Consciousness Movement underwent various rewritings during performances before the final print publication (Gilbert, 2007: 13). However, dramatic and performance theories "have much to offer post-colonial debates about language, interpellation, subject-formation, representation, and forms of resistance" (Gilbert & Tompkins, 1996: 9). The difficulty, if not impossibility, of national audiences, let alone foreign drama enthusiasts, of actually viewing a live performance of contemporary drama, need not, and should not, prevent the study and criticism of this highly immediate and provocative genre. Postcolonial theatre critics tend to focus on what Femi Euba argues is an excessive interest in oppression and resistance, which "has tended to obfuscate other developments of political theatre in Africa" (Euba, 2002: 671). This is, of course, a valid argument as theatre, in our case South African, tends to be neglected in most postcolonial criticism as Gilbert and Tompkins point out. The question is whether we should be analyzing South African literature – and more specifically, Indian South African theatre – under the umbrella term of postcolonial writing. Loren Kruger claims that "the term 'postcolonial' and the sovereign state it presumably denotes has yet to gain the currency in South Africa that it enjoys in metropolitan academic circles" (1995: 61). Certainly, persisting class and ethnic inequalities suggest the truth of this statement but if we define the postcolonial moment as the demise of discriminatory racial laws and the achievement of universal franchise then post 1994 South Africa has indeed entered the postcolonial stage. So, why has South African postcolonial drama not received that much critical attention? To my mind, the problem resides not only in the discrepancies between the published text and the performance but in more far-reaching issues. While students around the world study Shakespeare's plays without ever having seen a live performance of the Bard's works, few university or secondary school teachers would include a contemporary play in their syllabi without the possibility of their students being able to see the acted performance of the drama in question. Obviously, factors surrounding the canon enter into this dilemma but we need to see performance as a tool of resistance to the inequalities of the status quo. Drama is an immediate and critical social self-introspection, and performance functions as a tool of resistance, but sadly economic questions of viability and the need for what actor and director Peter Hayes calls "a commercial edge" enter into the choice (Nuttall & Michael, 2000: 210). He argues that contemporary playwrights have to compete with sports events and more popular understandings of culture when it comes to corporate sponsors. This suggests that thought-provoking plays are – like literary novels – no longer on the popular agenda but our aim as critics is to vindicate the importance of serious drama – if by "serious" we mean plays that question our prejudices, our comfortable middle-class positions, and our stereotypical visions of the Other. Our duty as university lecturers is to promote this kind of drama, regardless of whether our students can attend a performance of the play, as drama is, and will always be, a reflection of our reality.

In this volume, we celebrate the work of Indian South African playwright Ashwin Singh, which, through its diversity of characters from all ethnic backgrounds, goes beyond the former resistance plays and forges a more inclusive South African identity. This does not mean to say that his plays cover up the race and class inequalities that still plague the nation. On the contrary, Singh's work is an attempt to bring these blatant prejudices and social ills to the forefront as only by confronting unpleasant realities can any far-reaching changes ever take place. Singh admirably fills in what Gilbert and Tompkins have called "the gap in post-colonial studies" (1996: 9) as his plays provide a sweeping overview of the trials and tribulations of the newly inaugurated post-apartheid, therefore postcolonial, state. The contrast between the climate of optimistic political protest and the complacency and disillusion of the new democratic era serves to reassess the actions of the past in the light of the present outcomes. *Into the Grey* (2017), Singh's most recently published play, spans over almost thirty years and, while not being totally pessimistic, does engage the audience to reflect on the actions of the heroes of the Struggle in the light of their current dubious choices. One of the many projects of postcoloniality is to review and rewrite past histories in order to present alternative viewpoints but also to reject any sense of the marginalized or colonized as having an inherent purity as opposed to the innate villainy of the colonizing white minority. Non-binary thinking is essential in any postcolonial reassessment of the past and Singh's plays avoid falling into this trap. His works encompass a myriad of current situations and social issues and he is careful to measure out dramatic moments with snatches of humour so the audience (or reader) can fully empathise with the characters.

In true theatrical fashion this volume is organized into three acts. Following this introduction, we provide a brief biography of the playwright and a list of his works. Act 1 concludes with an interview with Ashwin Singh which highlights his concerns with the future of contemporary South African theatre, which is witnessing rapidly diminishing theatre audiences. Despite competition from television, Netflix and the like, Singh claims that, like other well-known foreign playwrights who use humour in their work, "comedy with substance can be effectively used to heal some of the country's unfinished business" so he still believes in the role of theatre as a vehicle for social change.

Act 2 contains six essays by leading academics and cultural practitioners. Betty Govinden inscribes Singh's oeuvre within the traditions of South African literature and drama in her chapter "'The Cartography of Struggle' in South African Theatre, with Particular Reference to *Reoca Light* by Ashwin Singh". She emphasizes how South African plays – and Ashwin Singh's are no exception - are "impelled by a robust political will to overcome apartheid, and strong impulses to focus on the goals of common citizenship". Govinden centres the main body of her article on Singh's one-man play *Reoca Light*, which, she claims, illustrates the survival tactics of the indentured labourers and their descendants. Her detailed discussion of the play focuses on the numerous themes that *Reoca Light* brings to the fore, including home, identity, diaspora and of course spatial politics.

Deborah Lutge, in her chapter "Ashwin Singh: Egg or Chicken: A Writer/Director's Recipe in Interviews and Analysis", seeks to unravel what she calls the chicken and egg syndrome, by comparing opinions of various leading South African playwrights including Ashwin Singh himself. She claims that the work of the director is as far-reaching as the playwright's - hence her title - and which together forge an alliance that aims to uncover a past which can explain the meaning of our present existence. She argues that "the relationship between writer and director is a mutually influential one, and it is the critical detachment that is the key to a solid working relationship". Her chapter emphasizes how Singh's work is paramount in "globally connecting contexts, by inviting and encompassing multi-layered perspectives, acknowledging the shift away from tunnel world-views grown in isolation".

Coplen Rose's chapter "From Rockets to Robots: The Function of Science Fiction Icons in Ashwin Singh's *Duped*" examines this 2011 play as a clever mixture of satire and Science Fiction deployed by the playwright in order to explore apartheid's traumatic legacy. The chapter acknowledges the playwright's refusal to think in binary terms as "Singh's foray into the SF genre avoids creating a simple binary between explorer and the people under assessment by identifying both parties as members of the same nation". Rose concludes by stating that, in true Singh fashion, the play's message is a warning call that mutual distrust and self-interest among South Africans could be used to install sinister methods of control.

Shantal Singh provides a psychological perspective to Ashwin Singh's plays in her chapter "Exploring Trauma in Post-Apartheid South Africa as Experienced by Lead Characters in Ashwin Singh's Plays *Shooting*, *Beyond the Big Bangs* and *Into the Grey*". She examines the playwright's ability to "balance the emotion of trauma [in post-apartheid South Africa] while entertaining the audience". Shantal Singh argues that while other South African playwrights have tackled this highly sensitive area, Ashwin Singh is able to go one step further by delving into the "complexities and contradictions" of his characters, victims and perpetrators. In her chapter, which focusses on three of Singh's plays, she highlights the difficulty of achieving an equilibrium and portraying three-dimensional characters when themes of trauma are foregrounded.

Pranav Joshipura's chapter "Racial Conflict Presented Through the Plays of Indian South African Playwright Ashwin Singh" explores the background to Indian South African theatre. This timely contextualization of the role of Indian South

African playwrights in recent history paves the way for his analysis of Singh's work. Joshipura points out that Singh's plays "not only present problems the nation faces at micro level of their multiracial existence but also pose questions to the government regarding their intention of governing the nation" thus signalling the political role of the playwright and his interpellation of his audiences in this task. Joshipura concludes that "Ashwin Singh's plays enable readers and theatregoers to explore racial and class divisions in South Africa as well as providing solutions to end them".

The final chapter of Act 2 is dedicated to Singh's latest performed play *Into the Grey* (2017). Felicity Hand argues that this play has to be read as a call for resilience as a way for more positive, adaptable solutions to contemporary inequalities, which can serve as antidotes for more positive thinking and a clear determination to abandon, what Singh calls the "grey".

Act 3 begins with Ralph Lawson's views on the role of the director. In his chapter "A Director's Cut. Staging the Play", Lawson, who has collaborated with Ashwin Singh in numerous productions, reveals the dilemmas and quandaries of a theatre director. Focussing on three of Singh's plays, Lawson succeeds in enlightening audiences and readers on the crucial decisions that a theatre director must take as regards characters' psychology and motivations, without losing sight of what he calls the playwright's "pivotal idea". Lawson makes it clear what Deborah Lutge suggests in her chapter that playwright and director form a symbiosis that turns the theatrical event into a multifaceted experience.

The final scene in Act 3 of this volume is Pallavi Rastogi's "Afterword. How to Swing the Game of Life in South Africa", which sums up many of the issues dealt with in the preceding chapters but with a special focus on the play *Swing*. Rastogi highlights Singh's essential Durban identity, which is apparent in most of his plays as well as his constant experimentation with new forms and new approaches within the genre of drama. She centres her main argument on the play *Swing* (2015), which has not been discussed in detail by any of the preceding authors. *Swing*, Rastogi argues, exemplifies "the conflict between the coloured and the Indian communities who are unable to transcend their differences". The play switches back and forth from the apartheid days to the present through the narratives of the two characters, Samantha and her father. Without a clear-cut resolution, the play leaves the viewer/ reader wondering what the outcome will be - who will win the tennis match, Samantha, the coloured-Indian or Lerato Sibisi, the umZulu – but this is precisely the point, South Africa will be whatever the people make it.

This volume aims to celebrate the work of Ashwin Singh, a "brave new voice " as Pallavi Rastogi calls him, and to encourage readers, theatre-lovers, postcolonial specialists and other interested scholars around the world to discover his amazing gift and enjoy learning about the reality/ realities – Singh would be the first to acknowledge this plurality - of post-apartheid South Africa from his entertaining and thought-provoking plays.

Bibliography

Bose, Neilish (ed.) 2009. *Beyond Bollywood and Broadway. Plays from the South Asian Diaspora*. Bloomington: Indiana University Press.

Desai, Ashwin & Goolam Vahed, 2016. *The South African Gandhi. Stretcher-Bearer of Empire*, Stanford: Stanford University Press.

Dharwadker, Aparna. 1998. Diaspora, Nation, and the Failure of Home: Two Contemporary Indian Plays. *Theatre Journal*, 50 (1), March: 71-94

Euba, Femi, 2002. Review of *Drama for a New South Africa: Seven Plays*, Edited by David Graver. *Theatre Journal*, 54 (4), December: 671-672.

Gilbert, Helen (ed), 2007. *Postcolonial Plays. An Anthology*. London: Routledge.

Gilbert, Helen & Joanne Tompkins, 1996. *Post-Colonial Drama*. London: Routledge.

Hansen, Thomas Blom, 2000. Plays, Politics and Cultural Identity Among Indians in Durban, *Journal of Southern African Studies*, 26 (2), June: 255-269.

Kruger, Loren, 1995. The Uses of Nostalgia: Drama, History, and Liminal Moments in South Africa, *Modern Drama*, 38: 60-70.

Nuttall, Sarah & Cheryl-Ann Michael, 2000. Introduction: Imagining the Present. In: S. Nuttall & C-A. Michael (eds). *Senses of Culture. South African Culture Studies*. Oxford: Oxford University Press. 1-23.

Rastogi, Pallavi, 2008. *Afrindian Fictions. Diaspora, Race, and National Desire in South Africa*. Columbus: The Ohio State University Press.

Singh, Ashwin, 2013. *Durban Dialogues, Indian Voice. Five South African Plays*, Twickenham, UK: Aurora Metro Books.

Singh, Ashwin, 2017. *Durban Dialogues, Then and Now*, Twickenham, UK: Aurora Metro Books.

SCENE 2

Ashwin Singh's Biography

Ashwin Singh is an attorney, academic, playwright, director, actor and filmmaker. His plays have received national and international exposure, having travelled throughout South Africa as well as to India and London. *To House; Spice 'n Stuff; Shooting; Beyond the Big* Bangs; *Reoca Light* and *Into the Grey* are widely regarded as his seminal works. His first anthology of plays, *Durban Dialogues, Indian Voice. Five South African Plays* was published in 2013 by London-based Aurora Metro Books. His second anthology, *Durban Dialogues, Then and Now* was published by Aurora Metro Books in 2017. These books are being studied and/or referenced at a variety of universities in South Africa, Mauritius, India, Canada and Europe. Singh has also been published as a playwright in the collective anthologies, *New South African Plays* (Aurora Metro Books, 2006) and *The Catalina Collection* (Catalina UnLtd, 2013). There have been several presentations on his oeuvre at seminars and conferences in South Africa, India and Europe. Singh is also a published poet and academic author. His debut novel, *Shooting*, based on the play of the same title was published by MicroMega Publications in 2020.

Singh is a three-time national award winner via the PANSA Playreading Festival (the country's foremost playwriting contest) with his plays *To House* (2003); *Duped* (2005; earlier version); and *Reoca Light* (2012). He is also a respected stage and radio actor, having performed in a number of dramatic and comic productions. The stage productions include *Spice 'n Stuff, Marital Blitz, PopCom, Culture Clash, To House* and *Into the Grey*. The radio productions include *Psycho Art, Switch Hitch* and *GrandAsia Lodge*. His plays *Spice 'n Stuff* and *To House* have been adapted for radio on Lotus FM and SA FM respectively. Singh also played a lead role in award winning UK director James Brown's short film about child abuse, *One Wedding and A Funeral* and has just written and directed his debut documentary feature film about Indian identity entitled *The Cane Cutters' Transcendence*.

Singh is a former board member of the Catalina UnLtd Theatre Company and has been a script writing and business mentor for the Playhouse Company's development programmes over the past decade. The Singh Siblings (Pty) Ltd and the Playhouse Company have been the most prominent producers of Singh's works.

Ashwin Singh's Plays and Other Theatre Works

The Plays

To House (2003)

Spice 'N Stuff (2006)

Shoooting (2009)

Reoca Light (2010)

Duped (2011)

Marital Blitz (2011) [Co-Written With Kajal Maharaj And Nesan Pather]

Culture Clash (2012) [Co-Written With Edmund Mhlongo]

Beyond the Big Bangs (2013)

Swing (2015)

Into the Grey (2017)

The Sketch Comedy Shows

The Rainbow Indignation (2001) [Co-Written With Joe Carroll And Ivan Boniaszczuk]

The Looney Lahnee Show (2009) [Co-Written With Dhaveshan Govender]

Popcom (2012) [Co-Written With Kajal Maharaj And Nesan Pather]

Popcom 2 (2020)

To House; *Spice 'n Stuff*; *Reoca Light*; *Duped* and *Beyond the Big Bangs* were published in the individual anthology Singh, A. *Durban Dialogues, Indian Voice. Five South African Plays*. 2013. London: Aurora Metro Books.

Shooting; *Swing* and *Into the Grey* were published in the individual anthology Singh, A. 2017. *Durban Dialogues, Then and Now*. London: Aurora Metro Books.

To House was also published in the collective anthology Fourie, C.J. (ed). 2006. *New South African Plays* London: Aurora Metro Books.

Spice 'n Stuff was also published in the collective anthology Catalina UnLtd. 2013. *The Catalina Collection*. Durban: Catalina UnLtd.

Shooting was adapted into a novel and published by MicroMega Publications in 2020.

SCENE 3

An Interview with Ashwin Singh

Felicity Hand

FH. As a Indian South African playwright, to what extent do you feel expected to write about this community?

AS. I see myself as a child of the universe, having enjoyed eclectic life experiences. However, I fully acknowledge that I am Black; a South African; of Indian origin; and that the city that I most connect with is my birthplace and current home, Durban ... the city that is part of the Kingdom of the Zulu but also home to the largest number of people of Indian origin outside India.

I have been significantly influenced by the cultures of Africa and of the Indian sub-continent. This is unsurprising ... I live on the African continent. I enjoy the beauty, the complexity, the music, the literature, the food of my country and continent ... and I am Black, because as a boy I identified with the Struggle against apartheid and was part of youth movements fighting against the dehumanising system. I am also emotionally connected to the Indian subcontinent. I have family and friends there. I love Indian music, literature, dance, food ... and all those exuberant colours!

Due to the racist designs of the apartheid regime, I grew up in what could still be termed an "Indian district" and so was obviously exposed to numerous Indian cultural influences ... in my home, at the local temples, at our segregated schools ...

I want to write about Durban and its complex people. Therefore, it is logical that I would write a fair amount about the Indian community ... and it is fair that I am expected to write about this community. However, I believe that I have every right to include characters from other cultural backgrounds in my plays and that I must do so because the Indian community does not exist in a vacuum. Therefore, my plays have a diverse array of characters. Inevitably, there are characters from the Indian community ... but there are also characters from the Zulu nation as well as those from Durban's mixed race communities and occasionally there are White Afrikaans-speaking characters too.

FH. Twenty-five years after the demise of apartheid, racial issues still seem to dominate current South African plays. Do you feel under any sort of pressure to include characters from different racial backgrounds?

AS. I signed up for a non-racial, intercultural project in democratic South Africa ... but sadly, that project no longer exists, despite what some deceptive politicians publicly state. We still live in a racist country. Sometimes, this racism is overt ... particularly in ugly spats on social media ... but more often nowadays it is covert. And we cannot simply dismiss this as a few ignorant White people who are clinging onto archaic belief systems. There are many racist Black African and Indian people in South Africa. Furthermore, there is significant racism in many of our foundational institutions like schools, universities, hospitals, public companies and government agencies. So the apartheid mentality has not dissipated ... and it will remain with us until we truly engage in an honest way about the fact that we continue to use the social construct of race as a divisive factor.

So playwrights have to deal with racial conflict and institutionalised racism ... it is a lived reality. I have confronted these themes many times in my plays. A few ill-informed artists and critics have occasionally suggested that I have explored this theme a little too much but most people agree that I have to examine what is an integral part of our daily existence. Of course, if you look further afield at the US and Europe, racial and ethnic conflicts are dominant issues currently and storytellers from these places are regularly exploring these topics in their theatre pieces and films.

I therefore don't feel under any specific pressure to include characters from different racial backgrounds ... it is just something that I naturally do because, as I have articulated, we still classify people according to race and we are still living in a racist country. So if I wrote only about one so-called race group then I would not be presenting an accurate, layered picture about my city and my country.

FH. I hate to raise the age-old question of authenticity, but do you feel that other ethnic groups resent you portraying "their" community in what they may construe as being a negative light?

AS. There have been a few artists, critics and members of the theatre-going public who have suggested that I should write only about the Indian community because I have a nuanced understanding of this community ... after all, I am Indian, they say. This is a very narrow-minded view. To begin with, very few of these people actually understand how diverse the Indian community itself is ... having a variety of sub-cultures in respect of religion, language, rituals, family structure, values and class systems. They assume the community is homogeneous and therefore by living with some of the members of the community I must be able to present an accurate picture of that community. They contend that I will not be able to present a layered picture of other South African communities or other ethnicities because I am not one of those people. This sounds a lot like apartheid-speak to me. It is putting people into boxes again ... cultural censorship of the worst order.

I have friends from a variety of so-called race groups and ethnicities. I went to a multicultural university. I speak more than one South African language. I may live in what is predominantly an "Indian district" but there are Black African, mixed-race and a few White people living there too. I interact regularly with these people. I live and work in a city where I encounter a multiplicity of complex cultural phenomena on a daily basis. And I am an academic who conducts detailed research.

So of course, I am going to write about all our peoples ... and sometimes, some of them will be presented in a negative light, whatever the dominant aspect of their cultural influence. Fortunately, I believe that I present layered characters ... people who have quirks, inconsistencies and contradictions, so there are no one-dimensional villains.

I am happy to state that the aforementioned critics are a small minority. The vast majority of people with whom I have had substantial conversations about my work have no problem with me writing about people from different ethnicities to my own. I have also received very positive feedback about the Zulu and mixed-race characters I have written about ... although I don't recall any detailed analysis of the few White characters I have constructed.

FH. There have been a recent number of publications which challenge the historical role Gandhi was said to have played during the years he spent in South Africa. Has your work been at all influenced, perhaps unconsciously, by his legacy or by the need to question his importance for the Indian South African community?

AS. Most people with whom I have spoken about Gandhi are very positive in respect of his impact on both the Indian and Zulu communities in our province of KwaZulu-Natal. They contend that he inspired many people within those communities to fight against the injustices of apartheid through non-violent protest action. Of course, his granddaughter, Ela lives in my city and she is a prime example of his legacy – she is a gentle and generous soul who has campaigned tirelessly for peace and justice, in both apartheid and democratic South Africa. I believe that many of the writers of these recent publications have made shallow and overly harsh judgements of a clearly flawed young man. Gandhi himself acknowledged later in life that he had made many misjudgements and prejudicial assumptions in his young adulthood. Naturally, he acquired much greater wisdom through many complex life experiences. Two of our former prominent Judges and anti-apartheid activists, Albie Sachs and Zac Yacoob acknowledged that they had been racist young men because they had been indoctrinated into this prejudicial belief system. They unlearned these attitudes and beliefs as they interacted with people having different value systems. They grew into becoming more enlightened about the world they inhabited and became great thinkers and leaders.

Gandhi's belief in and struggle for equality and non-violence in the world has influenced my work. Many of my plays examine South Africa's culture of violence. Of course, apartheid was the foundation for this culture of violence but it is still prevalent after a quarter of a century of democracy. And we live in the most unequal society in the world. Lead characters in plays like *Reoca Light, Into the Grey, Shooting* and *Beyond the Big Bangs* cry out for greater honesty and urgency in the way that we are approaching this violent way of life as well as calling for more depth and innovation in our attempts to combat growing inequality.

FH. How do you see the future of theatre in contemporary South Africa? Do you think it can still create public opinion?

AS. In the first fifteen years of democracy, South African playwrights and theatre-makers continued our tradition of robust drama which fearlessly explored challenging socio-political issues, as had been courageously done by artists like Athol Fugard, John Kani, Mbongeni Ngema and Lewis Nkosi (to name a few) during the apartheid years. In the immediate post-apartheid world, there was very little censorship and therefore much greater freedom to examine a host of controversial issues, from inequality and racial discrimination to corruption and poor governance to the debilitating effects of violent crime.

However, the last decade has seen a significant diminishing of the impact and influence of theatre in South Africa, particularly in Durban. Due to economic factors, political instability, rising urban decay, and distractions like satellite television and the internet, we now have a rapidly diminishing theatre audience. Our Playhouses have also failed to build a young Black audience. Theatre on a Saturday night is simply not an enticing option for the vast majority of South Africans, across the cultural spectrum. This has had a ripple effect with artistic directors and independent producers putting on a lot more light comedy shows and musicals in their venues in order to stay afloat. We have also suffered reduced public funding so daring new works are few and far between. Many young writers and actors, unable to sustain a living from theatre, have turned to television soaps in desperation.

Interestingly, South Africa's film industry is gaining momentum and the government seems determined to offer innovative funding opportunities in this regard. We are still focused on narrow market factors however, therefore the majority of films made are for the popcorn brigade.

The above situation is reflective of world trends in theatre and film, although in several places in the world like London, New York, Chicago, Mumbai, Sydney, Tokyo, Toronto … there is still a theatre culture. Apart from Cape Town to some degree, the people entrusted with the administration of our theatre world don't seem to have a clue as to how we could try to build a theatre culture.

Yet I am still hopeful that theatre may not completely die and that some powerful theatre pieces may still create public opinion in South Africa. The reason for this optimism is that I have met so many passionate young artists, mostly Black African, who are so eager to write for and perform on our stages. I have mentored some of these multi-talented people on the Playhouse Company's development programmes and they have inspired me. They are determined to plough on. Perhaps they will, in time, build a brave new audience as well.

I also have to mention some of our stalwarts, who have resisted the temptations of commercial television series and films and continue to put their stories on the stage. The likes of Mike van Graan, Paul Slabolepszy, Mandla Mbotwe, Lara Foot, Sylvain Strike, Aubrey Sekhabi, Neil Coppen…are people of the theatre … this is the medium that they truly love…and they can still pull something of a crowd too!

FH. One thing that struck me about some of the recent South African plays I have seen is the juxtaposition of comical features and highly traumatic events. Would you say this is a very South African way of dealing with the horrors of the recent past? How do you feel about using comedy to heal some of the country's still unfinished business?

AS. Yes, this is a South African way of dealing with our horrific past … and our very challenging contemporary issues too! South African artists often use humour as a tool to explore a vast array of uncomfortable truths … and to examine sensitive issues. This is usually done with compassion and artistic nuance, although some artists with limited dramatic range and emotional depth, have presented uneven and superficial works. Pieter-Dirk Uys and Paul Slabolepszy have very powerfully constructed the juxtaposition of comical features and highly traumatic events in their works over the years.

I don't make a rigid distinction between comedy and drama. Life is full of moments of heightened drama or even tragedy followed quickly and strongly by therapeutic or even uncomfortable humour. If we are truly alive, then we cry and we laugh every day. Great drama often contains humorous moments just as great comedy is punctuated with moments of pathos.

South African theatre-makers have at times attracted larger audiences to works confronting dark and haunting themes through the clever and disarming use of humour. Many believe that humour can also be a vehicle for social change. I have often juxtaposed comical features and traumatic events in my plays, most significantly in *Shooting, To House, Duped* and *Beyond the Big Bangs*. I certainly believe that comedy with substance can be effectively used to heal some of the country's unfinished business.

I must hasten to add that while this juxtaposition may feature more in South African works, it is certainly used by some playwrights and film-makers overseas as well. Some of these artists have influenced my work as well, particularly David Mamet, Harold Pinter, David Lynch and the Coen brothers.

FH. You sometimes act in your own plays. Has this helped you to rethink some of your dramaturgical strategies?

AS. I think that it has been very useful for my artistic evolution that I am both a playwright and an actor. The two disciplines have different approaches and different energies. Writing is a more intellectual exercise, although one has to appeal to an audience's emotions as an author. Acting comes more from instinct and it is obviously a more physical activity than writing. Both activities require a substantial understanding of human behaviour.

When I write a scene, I then perform it to test if it sounds intellectually and emotionally appropriate. One hears a play (as one sees a film) so I believe that this exercise is critically important. I also ask other actors to perform pieces with me at various times in the play's development to complete this process. Therefore, the actor's input (including my input in that capacity) is an important development strategy which I employ. As a result of the aforementioned, performing in the final production on stage does not alter my perceptions too much. However, at various times during rehearsals, particularly with director Ralph Lawson (himself a fine actor), we have made cuts and little tweaks to the script because we have found some passages of some of my texts to be a little unwieldy or simply too verbose.

FH. What other South African playwrights have most influenced you? Are you all following similar trends?

AS. I have not been hugely influenced by South African playwrights. That is not to say that I do not respect and admire South African playwrights ... quite the contrary ... but I have followed my own path. I have to some degree been influenced by Athol Fugard, particularly with regard to language and the construction of character. In terms of structure and tone, American playwright (and screenwriter) David Mamet has had some influence on me.

Stylistically, I don't believe that the established South African playwrights are following similar trends. The younger playwrights however, are all quite significantly influenced by film ... and I would state that I am also influenced by art films. The younger Black African playwrights also seem to use music (and occasionally dance as well) in their works, sometimes effectively, sometimes not at all.

Thematically, the established playwrights still mainly create issue-driven plays, although with declining audiences, some have been tempted to try more frivolous comedies and musicals. The emerging playwrights fluctuate between light entertainment and more serious art. Many of the trainees I have mentored at the Playhouse Company have written works exploring very dark subject-matter.

Plays dealing with issues of race, class, growing inequality, government corruption, AIDS, identity politics and violent crime are still quite prevalent on South African stages. I have explored these themes in my plays as well.

FH. I was surprised to find out how short plays often run in South Africa. Is this solely due to economic factors or is there a lack of a consolidated theatre-going tradition. If so, what do you suggest could be done to create one?

AS. South Africa has major economic problems. Unemployment and poverty remain our biggest challenges, twenty five years into democracy. Most people simply cannot afford to go to the theatre. Most theatres are also located in the heart of our cities where there exists the real threat of violent crime. So it is cheaper and safer for people to watch movies in the mall ... or at home ... or simply to surf the web.

Economic factors definitely play a role in the shortening of theatre runs in many parts of South Africa, particularly in respect of plays. However, as I have previously indicated, we have failed to build a theatre audience in contemporary South Africa. During apartheid, many White people went to the theatre to see ballet and opera and occasionally a locally made play too. Many Black people also loved theatre but were forced to watch shows in their township halls. This proved very popular and playwrights like Gibson Kente and Ronnie Govender became local legends. This pastime has died out though. The Playhouses belong to everyone now so theatre in the communities is no longer appealing ... and of course, there are so many distractions and entertainment options now.

The government and big business also don't care about theatre. We are a sports obsessed nation...and huge money is poured into this while serious art forms like theatre, literature and the fine arts are ignored.

To be honest, I don't believe that the vast majority of South Africans care about the play as an art form...or as a genuine entertainment option anymore. If they want to consume live art, they would rather go to a stand-up comedy show or to a dance piece.

I believe that we have to work more closely with schools to build a storytelling and theatre culture. The Dramatic Arts is still a popular subject at school but we need co-ordinated programmes at local and national level between the Department of Arts and Culture, the Playhouses and our schools to stimulate creativity and a serious appreciation for the arts. We need more tours of theatres, more writing and acting workshops, more opportunities for young writers to get their works onto our stages. We need theatre craft to be taught better in our schools so that young people begin to truly appreciate the nuances of theatre.

We also need to include more local drama and fiction on our secondary school and university syllabi. Young people urgently need to discover more local characters and authentic African drama. The Playhouses also have to invest in a detailed, innovative process to develop more local writers who regularly create stories which speak to the lived reality of our multicultural world. And South African people have to relearn how to appreciate authentic South African work ... rather than cocooning at home watching stale American television.

FH. You are a qualified lawyer and yet you haven't written a courtroom play. Considering how successful this genre is in the US, why haven't you explored this area?

AS. I have seldom found courtroom dramas, whether on stage or screen, particularly engaging. I suppose the extent of the "artistic licence" utilised, so out of touch with actual courtroom procedures, has irritated me. I can understand why people may find the process, in artistic form, quite enthralling but it does not stimulate me. I also think that there has been an over-proliferation of courtroom dramas on American television, exported to the wider world, so the form is becoming tiresome.

That is not to say that I have found practising as a lawyer in court uninspiring. It is very challenging, intellectually stimulating and at times pretty entertaining too! It is just that the bulk of the work is done before you enter the court and the world of drama has tended to distort this fact to the point of farce.

I must also point out that I have featured lawyers as lead characters in some of my plays (*To House, Spice 'n Stuff, Shooting* and *Into the Grey*) and have examined their professional world in some detail. Therefore, it is clear that my career in law has impacted on my artistic explorations.

FH. Some Indian or African authors provide a glossary for non English terms or even ways of pronunciation. Have you ever considered doing this as some of your characters use isiZulu or Afrikaans words and expressions? I must admit that as a non-South African, these glossaries do come in very handy. What are your views on this? Are you saying that South Africa is by nature a polyglot nation? So should the non-South African reader or theatre goer just have to work it out from the context?

AS. I did include a glossary in the educational edition of my first anthology, *Durban Dialogues, Indian Voice* but my publishers and I decided not to include a glossary in the main editions of both anthologies. The educational edition is aimed at secondary school pupils and we felt that they would require a glossary. We believed that mature readers (who would use the main editions) whether South African or not, would understand the language in context. We have not as yet done an educational edition for the second anthology, *Durban Dialogues, Then and Now* because schools are still using the first anthology and will only get to the second anthology after several years.

South Africa has eleven official languages but the fact is that it is mainly Black African people who fluently speak an African language. Due to apartheid, most people over 40 would have been forced to learn Afrikaans at school and so many people in this demographic would have some proficiency in that language, along with English of course. Younger people would have been exposed to their regional

African language at school but the reality is that English remains the language of commerce, science and the arts.

So it would be inaccurate to suggest that South Africa is a polyglot nation. Given this contention and the fact that my anthologies will have many readers from other countries, it would perhaps be advisable that future editions of the books (whatever the version) include a glossary.

ACT 2

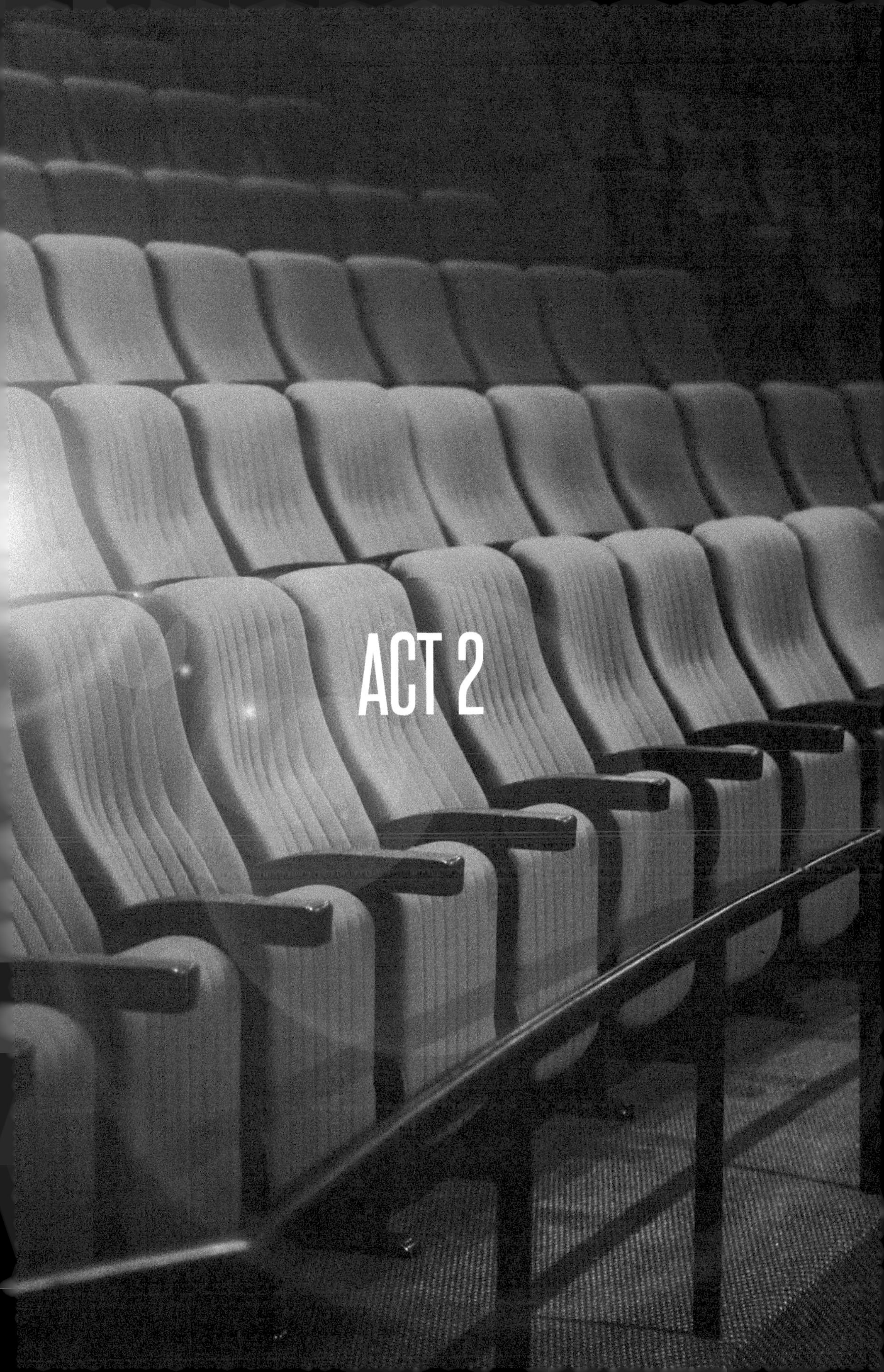

SCENE 1

'The Cartography of Struggle' in South African Theatre, with Particular Reference to *Reoca Light* by Ashwin Singh

Betty Govinden

Literature as a Mirror to Society

If literature holds up a mirror to society, nowhere is this truer than in South Africa. South African literature, from colonial times, and especially through the apartheid era, has shown up the society to itself. The watershed events of South African history after 1948, when the National Party came into power - the Sharpeville Massacre in 1961, the Soweto Riots in 1976, and Steve Biko's assassination in 1977, to name a few – all served, especially, to influence the output of literary writings in different genres, and also determine the direction of the writings.

South African theatre has particularly played this critically reflective role in the context of our history. The key plays in South African theatre have all zeroed in on living under apartheid - Fugard's *Blood Knot* (1961) and *Boesman and Lena* (1969), *Woza Albert* (1983) by Mbongeni Ngema, Percy Mtwa and Barney Simon, and Fugard, John Kani and Winston Ntshona's *Sizwe Bansi is Dead* (1972), to quote a few well-known examples.

Key Plays in Indian South African Theatre

Indian South African writing in general, and drama in particular, has also highlighted life and living in South Africa, with particular attention to the specificities of separate living, culture, language, histories, in their relationships in the broader society. An intrinsic part of Black writing and the arts in general, it has aimed at inclusivity, featuring various configurations of relationships among racial groups, and exploring a variety of themes pertinent to apartheid living.

In his excellent critical study of drama in India and the Indian diaspora, Neilesh Bose (2009) has examined a cross-section of plays across continents. Important plays in the tradition of Indian South African theatre, noted by Bose, are *The Lahnee's Pleasure* (1972), by Ronnie Govender [a play about racial and class discrimination, and white privilege], *Working Class Hero* (1970s), by Kessie Govender, where we see the intersection of class and race, and Kriben Pillay's *Waiting for Muruga* (1990), which also depicts similar themes. Bose astutely highlights a variety of aesthetic, ideological and political considerations that the plays dramatise.

There are also many plays, since the mid-1960's, by Black Consciousness playwrights such as Sam Moodley, Strini Moodley, Saths Cooper, Asha Moodley, Benjy Francis, and Mafika Gwala, which have had a major impact on the way South African society has been portrayed and its politics contested (see Moodley, 2018).

"Indian" in South Africa

Plays in South Africa invariably mirror a land "burdened by race", to use the title of Mohamed Adhikari's book on coloured identities in Southern Africa (2009). The racialisation of people in South Africa, and the demarcation of "population groups" is a long and convoluted story. apartheid legislation designated four groups – Whites, Africans, Coloureds and Indians - but the vexed anomalies of such a racial classification have been all too evident over the years. For example, there has been much contestation over the question of "Indian" identity in South Africa, and of Coloured, for that matter. Shireen Hassim has pointed out that one common way of looking at Indians and Coloureds "is to place them in an in-between space" (Hassim, 2019:9). However, as she argues, looking at the work of someone like Fatima Meer, Indians in South Africa, as with other Black groups, were not necessarily dogged by feelings of liminality (Hassim, 2019:10).

Plays in South Africa depict the pervasive racialised attitudes and behaviours on a broad spectrum, from the conservative to the radical. While apartheid tended to homogenise groups and emphasise difference, many of the plays are impelled by a robust political will to overcome apartheid, and strong impulses to focus on the goals of common citizenship.

Theatre – as a Political Space for Critical Exchange

In his analysis of Gibson Kente's plays, Rolf Solberg, the Norwegian critic, well-versed in South African Black theatre, argues that it is important to remember that Black Consciousness had its beginnings in intellectual circles, among students and academics, and that it took some time for strategies and modes of expression to catch on in the streets. He states that, consequently, and referring in particular to Matsemala Manaka's plays, "township audiences were not sufficiently attuned to the argumentative, highly politicised mode of Black Consciousness theatre" (Solberg, 2011: 53).

Kente, for his part, is criticised for his leading characters coming across as a little "moralistic, theatrically 'indigestible', inclined to sermonise" (Solberg, 2011:25), and somewhat "cerebral". I do not agree with this point of view and have found, from my personal experience, being a regular theatre-goer for decades, that

South African plays, in a variety of forms and shapes, have generated a healthy debate across the social spectrum. And the audiences, particularly attuned to a history of mass gatherings and political speeches, warm to the "speeches" that generally tend to be an important part of the texture of our plays.

In South Africa, generally speaking, going to the theatre is not a casual outing, to pass the time, or to search for entertainment. It is an act of protest and of solidarity - a political act, an intellectual exercise. Plays tacitly open up, as with cultural studies in general, "a discourse about publics and new intellectual spaces" (see Nuttall & Michael, 2000:14). As far as plays go, in particular, South Africans place great value on seeing portrayals on stage of the realities of living in South Africa – our histories, dilemmas and challenges, hopes and fears, contradictions.

There is much prompting, by the plays themselves, to extend the analyses and critique, to engage in debate about the plays' messages, and to perpetually re-focus the angle of vision presented on past and current political and social realities. This is true of most South African plays, and the plays of Indian South African writers are no exception. Decades ago, Black Consciousness activist, and former Robben Islander, Saths Cooper, produced *Antigone* in Durban, and literally suspended the play in mid-stream, to engage in a direct and open debate with the audience. The Greek play was also used by Athol Fugard, as a play-within-a play, in *The Island* (1973). In Cooper's production, the spontaneous, unscripted exchange was part of the performance. Predictably, the discussion was steered towards a consideration of confrontation with the state – a key issue which the Sophocles play highlights – and there was ready participation from the audience, once they realised what was happening.

Do the plays change anything? They certainly increase the level of debate, and of self-reflection. There is usually much discussion and debate around the plays that are on the circuit, both in public and private spaces. I would argue that this certainly changes perceptions and opinions, and the reflections and critique of South African society generated by the plays influence how we think and how we live. Presciently, in Fugard's play, *The Coat* (1977), a character says: "We want to use theatre. For what ... ? Some of us say to understand the world we live in, but we also boast a few idealists who think that theatre might have something to do with changing it" (Gray, 1990:53).

Post-apartheid Theatre

This tendency – of turning the gaze inwards - has continued into the post-apartheid era, as one of the most important aspects of living in South Africa is trying to understand our history, to deal with its enduring effects, particularly its racism and consequent inequities in our present lived contexts, in our striving to become a truly non-racial, democratic nation. Interestingly, South Africa is described as "a recited society", to use de Certeau's (1984:186) words, and this has increased exponentially since 1994, with radio talk shows, Letters to the Editor, social media, book launches, and stand-up comedy, as well as informal conversations across dinner tables in South Africa, being among the familiar spaces in which the current society is dissected and contested relentlessly. Arjun Appadurai has commented on the role of social media, for one, on everyday social life and on the imagination itself (Appadurai 1996; In Nuttall & Michael 2000:15). Indeed, this very appearance of a post-apartheid pluralism shows how far we are from a shared utopia that was dreamed of during the dark days of apartheid (Nuttall & Michael, 2000:54). Part of the process of endemic scrutiny, as before, is through literary writing, and dramatic performance in the theatre, in the attempt to lay bare, in various configurations, the polemics of our context.

Ashwin Singh's Plays

This is where Durban playwright Ashwin Singh's plays insert themselves, as they reflect South African realities, and generate discussion and reflection and debate on the past as well as the present. While we have had many retrospectives of plays since 1994, which have appeal for their recalling of the bad old days of apartheid now being received and pondered over in a different, changed moment, Singh's plays are relatively new. They speak to our contemporary situation, in their scrutiny of South African society, at the same time that they recall the old histories. In this respect a good example in Singh's oeuvre is the play *Reoca Light*.

Reoca Light - Background

Reoca Light, which has one person playing multiple roles, covers a wide spectrum of aspects and issues. It is set in Reoca, in Durban, described as "the People's City", and as sub-Saharan Africa's largest port city (see Maylam and Edwards, 1996). Reoca sounds like a version of Avoca, an actual suburb in Durban, which was developed for Indians during the apartheid era when "Group Areas" legislation was in operation and where, incidentally, Singh himself lives. The townships in Durban – Lamontville, Cato Manor, Wentworth, Chatsworth, Umlazi, KwaMashu, Inanda, and Clermont – dotted around the city - are a defining part of the spatial planning of the apartheid past. Reoca is a fictional, imagined place, created by Singh, but it is an accurate representation of the structure, aesthetics, people and events of one of the Indian townships designed by the apartheid regime.

If Reoca was *territorialised* in a certain way during apartheid, with particular ethnic significations, it is now being *reterritorialised* in diverse ways, as Singh shows so adeptly, as the new collides with the old in the same physical space. Singh renders this social space as a microcosm of South Africa. Sean Field, Meyer and Swanson

(2007: back cover) have drawn attention to the fact that cities are more than just "buildings and roads – they are also constructed through the popular imagination and spaces of representation". And as John Clement Ball observes: "It has been said that a city is a text – one that can, like a novel or film, be read for its stories and histories, for the ideologies it reflects and the power relations it inscribes" (Ball, 1996: 9). This description, about London, is, arguably, apt here as well. The play, *Reoca Light*, is set against the background of Indian Indenture, and combines this history from over 150 years ago, to events in the past decades before 1994, and into the present time.

The play begins with Areendum Rastogi, centre stage, an indentured labourer in the canefields of Natal around the 1870s. His opening speech, to the faint strains of Indian music, alludes to the sparse, peasant fare of their lives, relations with his white employer to whom he and his wife, Pallavi, are indentured, and his ultimate dreams of creating a better life for himself by becoming a store owner. Merely ten years since the arrival of his fellow indentured Indians to Natal, Rastogi is quite categorical that returning to India is not an option: "We can't go back to India, Biswas. This is our home" (RL 164).

Against this epigraph, Rastogi's great, great grand-son, Sunil, a fourth-generation family member, is inside his father's shop, at the present time, in conversation with a reporter, who has come in search of stories of the past. It is evident that Rastogi's dream of owning his own store had been realised. The irony, of course, is that this position is now seen as being low on the social ladder by some of his contemporaries, and Sunil is taunted for this: "My father is an engineer. Your father is just a shopkeeper" (RL 169). However, there have been recent attacks on the shop, and the recounting of the incidents to the reporter gives Sunil a chance to remember, to recall the past from different angles. We are soon aware of the intersections of histories and experiences in this smorgasbord of apartheid and post-apartheid life.

Sunil tells the story behind the store and, along the way, of the three men who most influenced his life (RL 168). One is Themba Dlamini, an African gardener, with whom a young impressionable Sunil develops a close bond. Themba brings with him his rich world of ancient myths and legends, his distinctive cuisine, and his self-taught skills, such as playing cricket at a time when South African national sports teams excluded Blacks. One sees the joyful "intimacy of strangers", to use the title of Judith Coullie's book (2001). These are people juxtaposed in the same space, building community naturally and spontaneously beyond the artificial barriers of class and race, age and aspiration. This was after Themba was left homeless, having had an unfortunate experience in Reoca, where another couple, Mr and Mrs Singh, wrongly accused him of stealing.

The other persons with whom Sunil had a close connection are his Uncle Johnny and his Dad. And the stories he recounts around them show infidelities and indiscretions; but worse than this, is the endurance of patterns of prejudice around religion, language differences and class, within groups, and now practised by some of the younger generation. Any resistance is met with disapproval: "You are interfering with the order of things, little man. This is the way of life in Reoca. A tradition and value system that spans generations" (RL 179).

And the rest of the play, through the storytelling, is an attempt to show the different challenges, vicissitudes, triumphs, betrayals, and acts of resilience of Rastogi's descendants and their compatriots, locked in love and locked in combat, learning to live in the world of Reoca - an allotment that can be as restricting or as expansive as you deem it to be. Sunil had written many of these stories already – as memory of the past is valued - and they now gradually unfurl, prompted as he is by the news reporter. And as the play proceeds, we see one story nesting in an earlier story, as with a Russian doll. All in all, we see the connected and competing stories in a complex web of entanglement, as the play dramatizes many of the key issues of living in post-apartheid South Africa.

One Person - Multiple Roles

In *Reoca Light*, the whole play is performed by one person, taking on and switching to different roles. This has great dramatic effect, with the versatility of the actor coming to the fore, and the action and plot of the play being advanced by the story-telling and through inference. The discursive undertones of this technique are worth considering. After all, we are all performing identities, as Judith Butler (1990) has argued in relation to gender. Arguably, this dramatic device suggests the arbitrariness, fluidity and elasticity of identities; yet, ironically, rigid social arrangements and oppressive social engineering are built on assumptions of fixed identities, as they were in apartheid. Further, in my opinion, this feature of the play has the effect of extended and shared remembering, through story-telling, as the sole actor gets under the skin of a variety of persons and identities, inhabits different lives, and presents shared histories and vignettes from diverse, individual vantage points. Shantal Singh (2013:19) points out that "*Reoca Light* is perhaps Singh's best tribute to the art of traditional story-telling."

What does it mean to inhabit another body? What does it mean to cross barriers and recall the memories of others in a country that gave us separate histories, separate memories? It is instructive to understand different identities, especially in a country where identity was prescribed and fixed in a deterministic way, and all boundary crossings were forbidden by apartheid law. What we have, at the end, from one body - but different voices - are intricate, and competing interpretations and narrations of experiences, from diverse perspectives and vantage points; all part of the warp and weft of the same polyphonic history, that is refracted in *Reoca Light*.

This dramatic device also has the effect of presenting a history from below, of portraying the ordinary, or subaltern voice, as Njabulo Ndebele has encouraged (1986), rather than the grand narratives of South African history. As Ndebele has observed: "[t]he history of Black South African Literature has largely been the history of the representation of spectacle... It is no wonder then, that the Black writer, sometimes a direct victim, sometimes a spectator, should have his imagination almost totally engaged by the spectacle before him" (1986:143).

In *Reoca Light*, Singh writes of the everyday and immediate, of what happens in the backyard of history. If there was a struggle, it was not the grand narrative of the Liberation Struggle as it is normally recounted. Support for it, of course, is given, if tangentially, surreptitiously, when, in the play, an activist is granted refuge from the apartheid police; but more than this, it is about the ordinary, everyday struggles to survive, to overcome daily indignities, and to defeat those who inflict them.

A Broad Discursive Landscape

It is clear that Singh's plays in general, and *Reoca Light* in particular, then, highlight some of the general discourses in South African cultural critique. Implicit in the play is a meshwork of discourses around entanglement, diaspora, memory, home and belonging, the politics of identity, among others. These are all, incidentally, quite familiar in critical discursive work in South Africa and beyond, and I consider a few here. I don't think that Singh himself is writing to any critical check-list. He is, I imagine, rather, working intuitively and rationally, from observation, experience and reflection; but it is quite instructive to see the connections and linkages here, and the way the same themes emerge in South African writings from different contexts and nodes of experiences.

Entanglement

Reoca, in *Reoca Light*, may be described, principally, as a crossroads, a place of interweaving, of entanglement. Sarah Nuttall states that, ironically, whether we acknowledge it or not, we are all – different race groups, different individuals – co-existing in a space of entanglement. She draws attention to the notion of "terrains of mutuality", and expounds on our historical, temporal, genetic and racial entanglement (Nuttall, 2009:6). This space of entanglement, prompts one to think of various possibilities in dealing with the realities of our divided history and the challenges towards reconciliation and integration. J. U. Jacobs, in his book, *Diaspora and Identity in South African Fiction* (2015), focussing on South African writers and critics, points out that entanglement is seen as a means by which "to draw into our analyses those sites in which what was once thought of as separate – identities, spaces, histories – come together or find points of intersection in unexpected ways" (Nuttall, 2009:11; Jacobs, 2016:3). In *Reoca Light*, we see the characters in various configurations of entanglement, both enabling and disabling. Some, of course, are better able than others to invoke the possibilities for community, and to seek ways to reconcile differences wrought by history.

A Sense of History

For all the characters, in different ways, there is a sense of history, an inescapable sense of the past. Here, in this play, the background history is of Indian indenture and of apartheid. And it is important to see this as part of the South African grand narrative. The play starts with the assertion of roots in indentured history, of a past that is lived with and recounted daily, and this provides the backdrop of the play, framing the action as it does.

Joan Chittister, a Benedictine nun, based in the United States, says that the past is both strange and interesting. "… The past is never really past … we live with it every minute of every day of our lives" (Chittister & Williams, 2011: Audio recording). And this is certainly true of the way indenture lives on in the psyche and memory of Indians in South Africa, as a compelling and inescapable residue. It is well-known now that traumatic historical events continue to have a lasting imprint, long after they have occurred, on those connected to them, and on their descendants. This is certainly true of slavery, indenture and the Holocaust, among other similar events. The spectre of the occurrence continues to constitute a "haunting capital", to use the title of Hershini Bhana Young's book (2006), This is evident quite starkly in the play, *Reoca Light*, where the history of indenture provides an essential backdrop, and is remembered and recounted, right up to the present time, compounded by other pressing contemporary vicissitudes that take centre stage.

Indentured labourers came to South Africa from 1860 to 1911, from the north and south of India. A total of 384 ships came from Madras and Calcutta, the main departure ports. In the 1870s and 1880s the Passenger Indians travelled from India, mainly from Gujarat, and sought business opportunities in the wake of the labourers' arrival. Gandhi was a significant arrival during this time, and lived in South Africa for 21 years, leaving a lasting legacy of civil disobedience, which defined the political struggles against apartheid during the 20th Century. Avoca, which mirrors Reoca in the play, is not too far from the Phoenix Settlement, where Gandhi's Ashram was established. It is a common feature of South African life to commemorate various national events, and the arrival of indentured Indians figures among them.

Diaspora

Against the background of Indian indenture, and attempts to adapt to a strange environment, individual lives took different trajectories. Out of the experiences of migration, and relocation from a homeland, for example, Indian, African, Chinese, among others, at different points in history a particular discursive diaspora poetics has emerged. This poetics of dislocation and displacement, sometimes referred to as *the diasporic imaginary* (Mishra, 2007), is reflected in the literature and arts of diasporas. Indian Diaspora literature has emerged from the broad historical forces of indenture, but also from particular local realities, and this is particularly evident in South African literature and the arts. This literature has emerged spontaneously on the soil of the adopted homeland, generally focussing on local issues, rather than on writing back to the homeland. This is certainly true of Indian South African literature, in particular, as I argue in my book, *Sister Outsiders* (see Govinden 2008), where the issues of living under apartheid are of all-consuming concern.

Reoca Light is a good example here, as are the other plays mentioned above. Singh's writings, as with diasporic and immigrant writing everywhere, are invariably about the politics of home and of identity, of a sense of belonging, exacerbated in South Africa with its past segregation laws. But, interestingly, in *Reoca Light* there is another layer of diasporic, or dispersed, living – within post-apartheid South Africa itself. It is also an attempt to critique and transcend the rigid compartmentalised living of the apartheid era:

> You know it's funny, my parents, like so many Indians, are moving to a formerly white suburb. But the other day, I saw a white couple moving into Reoca. And two black families moved here last year. Now this side is that side; our side is their side; their side is everybody's side. There are no boundaries. (RL 185)

A Time of Memory

Invariably, then, and as alluded to already, the present period becomes a time of memory, where the past is recounted, from different vantage points, to understand the present. Remembering the apartheid past, for example, shows the horrors of segregation: [Zaakir, an activist, tells Sunil in 1988] "One day you'll play chess with a grandmaster. And you won't play cricket behind your shop. Unless you want to. You will be playing cricket at The Wanderers" (RL 167).

The apartheid past, as depicted in the play, is also about the world of informers - "I don't know to this day who had ratted him out" (RL 167) - and of collaborators, like Pappa Singh, who supported the Tricameral Parliament (RL 168). As Hannah Arendt has observed, controversially, in *Eichmann in Jerusalem*, the Holocaust would not have been possible without the help of the Jewish councils (see Gessen, 2018: 6). In *Reoca Light* we see the indignity encountered by domestic employees, their unfair dismissal, and the violation of their fundamental rights. There was the unconscionable dismissal of Themba by the Singhs, referred to earlier, with Themba immediately suspected of stealing. The racial prejudice of yesteryear is palpable.

Remembering also contributes to re-membering, of stitching together, and repairing. Ngugi states in *Re-membering Africa* (2009) that much of the struggle in Africa has been about overcoming destruction and dispossession and building anew. Indeed in *Reoca Light*, remembering leads to re-membering and restoration, through redemption, as hope is reaffirmed.

Place

All the impulses outlined so far are played out in a place, this being a defining feature of writing in South Africa in general, as mentioned earlier, and of *Reoca Light*, in particular. Writers are conscious of place as the theatre of living in South Africa, each with a similar and different value in our collective memory, our collective psyche, our history, both local or national. Place, in South African writing is indeed where a variety of cultures and histories are simultaneously affirmed and subverted, and identities made and unmade. Indeed, all the issues around freedom, identity, morality, difference are played out in Singh's play from different vantage points[2] in the single place called Reoca. Reoca, like so many places in apartheid South Africa, is both the place of difference, and also the place where affinities are sought or created. Similarly, the play, *At the Edge*, by Ronnie Govender (1996)[3], depicts Cato Manor in its diversity, decades ago, while Durban's Casbah, its surface and its underbelly, comes alive in its "infinite variety", in the novel *The Lotus People*, by Aziz Hassim (2002). Through these places, and what they symbolise, and through writings on these places in South Africa, we have all lived in Reoca, or Cato Manor, or the Casbah - or Sophiatown or District Six, or Soweto for that matter - and we all identify with the reality of life in these places. Such identification, evoked by drama that is created from these spaces, becomes a political act.

Singh, through his various plays, maps out this "cartography of struggle"[4], implicitly showing the relationality between place and struggle, and the variegated drama of living in South Africa, in all its hopes and possibilities, traversing this landscape both physically and emotionally and mentally, and identifying with it closely. Among his other plays, *Spice 'N Stuff* is set in Grey Street, a trading district

---

2   See Worden , 1995
3   The date corresponds to the publication of the collection of short stories *At the Edge and Other Cato Manor Stories*, 1996. Pretoria: Manx
4   See Alvarez. 2018

in the city of Durban. *Duped* is set in the Airship Equity and the Durban CBD. *To House* is set in Oaklands, a middle-class suburb in the city of Durban and *Beyond the Big Bangs* in a middle-class suburb in Durban North.

The places in these plays have socio-historical significance; they are, in their different ways, part of the economy of injustice, as they denote segregated living, or are the site of apartheid atrocities, or global injustice. They are also the theatre of inter-group living, with all its tensions and striving and struggle for camaraderie and community. Singh, and the characters in his plays, are also rooted in these places - this is where they belong. This is who they are. Place defines them. This is where they find their identity. And it is an identity in a collective space, in apartheid's separate spaces, and in a longing to transcend the confines of these spaces.

This impassioned longing is evident in this excerpt from Antjie Krog's poem, "Country of Grief and Grace", in her collection, *Down to my Last Skin - Poems* (Krog, 2000)

> *between you and me*
> *how desperately*
> *how it aches*
> *how desperately it aches between you and me*
> *how long does it take*
> *for a voice*
> *to reach another*
> *in this country held bleeding between us…*

Space

Space, alongside place, is an important denominator in South African writings. Where, in a place, do things mainly happen? In South African Black writing these spaces may include hostels, yards, streets, shebeens, trade union halls - spaces that were directly linked to the realities of apartheid living (Sitas, 2015:82). These spaces, otherwise nondescript spaces, become spaces of consequence. In *Reoca Light*, the hut behind the shop is the unlikely space where so much of the drama takes place. The hut is where the family began informal trading, and they kept the hut even after they acquired the shop.

This hut began as their little shop, at the back of their home, where they sold their murkoos and sweets, to augment their income. All Sunil's great, great grandfather managed was a little stand:

He built a little stand and sold his food from there. Chappaties, mielie-meal roti, all kinds of fritters. He sold to his people. And to his oppressors. He never got the shop he wanted. But he carried on anyway. (RL185)

> Sunil recalls that they once hid one of the liberation activists, Zaakir Ally, in the hut, and that he was there when the police raided the place. It was the space where he spent precious time with the activist, who became his friend, listening to his stories, or learning to play chess. Paradoxically, this very space, hidden from view, is the centre of much of the action. The hut was the place where Sunil enjoyed close camaraderie with Themba, sharing in his stories of his village. "The hut where I savoured my mother's murkoos, was now filled with the delicious smells of sausage and pap. And after supper Themba would tell me stories of his village" (RL171). This is something of the light of Reoca, in an otherwise dark world.

The hut is also the place for the secret rendezvous for star-crossed lovers, forbidden by prejudice from being together. But the hut becomes a forbidden space when, one day, Sunil discovers his father in the arms of Mrs Singh, from Reoca. Sunil is scandalised, and his father, repentant, wants to burn down the hut. But Sunil prevents this from happening: "Don't burn it. Let it stand. I'll always cherish the other things that happened in there. So much of my life story resides there" (RL 183). Indeed, our past is variegated and entangled, comprising the good and the bad.

Conclusion

Scene 8, which acts as the epilogue, of *Reoca Light* ends in the same spirit as the epigraph. A hundred and fifty years ago, it was hope that galvanised the newly-arrived. Now, in the present time, it is hope that is claimed, and hope that drives them on. Structurally and thematically, across the span of time and consequence, there is unity in the play. Areendum Rastogi is back, centre stage.

> How can you say your life has meant nothing, Biswas? What is your legacy? I'll tell you what. A legacy of hope … We must shout to the world – I, Areendum, with my wife Pallavi, and my friend Biswas, came to this unknown land. We were fooled by selfish, savage people. They tried to make us forget who we were. But we didn't forget. We survived. We grew. We dreamed. And we did something. This is our home. (RL 185-6)

Life has come full circle, and it is time for an intermission.

Bibliography

Adhikari, Mohamed. (ed). 2009. *Burden by Race – Coloured Identities in Southern Africa*. Cape Town: UCT Press.

Alvarez, Sandra C, 2018. "Tracing a Cartography of Struggle: Reflections on Twenty Years of Transnational Solidarity with the U'wa People of Colombia." *International Feminist Journal of Politics,* 20 (1): 86-90.

Ball, John C. 1996. "The Semi-Detached Metropolis - Hanif Kureishi's London." *ARIEL – A Review of International English Literature*, 27 (4), October: 7-27.

Bhana Young, H. 2006. *Haunting Capital –Memory, Text, and the Black Diasporic Body*. Hanover, New Hampshire: Dartmouth College Press.

Bose, Neilesh. (ed). 2009. *Beyond Bollywood and Broadway – Plays from the South Asian Diaspora*. Bloomington, US: Indiana University Press.

Chittister, Joan. & Williams, Rowan. 2011. *Uncommon Gratitude – Alleluia for all that is*. Cincinatti, Ohio: St Anthony Messenger Press. Audio Recording.

Butler, Judith. 1990. *Gender Trouble: Feminism and the Subversion of Identity*. New York:Routledge.

de Certeau, M. 1984. *The Practice of Everyday Life*. Stanford: Stanford University Press.

Coullie, Judith L. (ed). 2001. *The Closest of Strangers – South African Women's Life Writing*. Johannesburg: Wits University Press.

Field, Sean., Meyer Renate. & Swanson, Felicity. (eds). 2007. *Imagining the City – Memories and Cultures in Cape Town*. Cape Town: HSRC Press: Back Cover.

Gessen, Masha. 2018. "To be, or Not to Be." *The New York Review of Books*, February 8, 2018, LXV, (2): 4-7.

Gray, Stephen. (ed). 1990. *My Children! My Africa! And Selected shorter plays*. Johannesburg: Wits UP.

Gikandi, Simon. 1996. *Maps of Englishness: Writing Identity in the Culture of Colonialism*. New York: Columbia University Press.

Govinden, Devarakshanam. 2008. *Sister Outsiders – The Representation of Identity and Difference in Selected Writings by South African Indian Women*. Pretoria: University of South Africa Press. Leiden:Koninklijke NV.

Govinden, Devarakshanam Betty. 2008. *A Time of Memory*. Durban: Solo Collective.

Hassim, Shireen. 2019. *Fatima Meer – A Free Mind*. Cape Town: HSRC Press.

Jacobs, Johan. 2015 *Diaspora and Identity in South African Fiction*. Scottsville: UKZN Press.

Krog, Antjie . 2000. *Down to My Last Skin*. SA: Random House.

Lamming, George. 1953. *In the Castle of My Skin*. London: Michael Joseph.

Maylam, Paul. & Edwards, Iain. (eds). 1996. *The People's City – African Life in Twentieth-Century Durban*. Pietermaritzburg: University of Natal Press.

Mphahlele, Es'kia. 1984. *Afrika my music* . Kwela Books: Cape Town.

Ngugi, wa Thiongo. 2009. *Re-membering Africa*, Nairobi, Kenya: East Africa Educational Publishers.

Mishra. Vijay. 2007. *Literature of the Indian Diaspora – Theorising the Diasporic Imaginary*. London: Routledge.

Moodley, Sam. (ed). 2018. *Time to Remember - Reflections of Women from the Black Consciousness Movement*. Durban: Published by Women for Awareness.

Ndebele, Njabulo. 1986. "Rediscovery of the Ordinary – Some new writings in South Africa." In: *Journal of Southern African Studies*, 12, (2): 143-157.

Nuttall, Sarah. 2009. *Entanglement – Literary and cultural reflections on post-apartheid*. Johannesburg:Wits University Press.

Nuttall, Sarah. & Michael, Cheryl-Ann. (eds). 2000. *Senses of Culture*. Oxford: Oxford University Press.

Singh, Shantal, 2013. "Summary and Analysis." In: Singh, Ashwin. *Durban Dialogues, Indian Voice – Five South African Plays*. Twickenham, UK: Aurora Metro Books. 17-21.

Singh, Ashwin. 2013. *Reoca Light*. In: *Durban Dialogues, Indian Voice – Five South African Plays*. Twickenham, UK: Aurora Metro Books. 163-186.

Sitas, Ari. 2016. The Flight of the Gwala-Gwala Bird- Essays in Labour and Culture in KwaZulu-Natal. Cape Town: SAHO Publications.

Solberg, Rolf. 2011. *Bra Gib – Father of South Africa's Township Theatre*. Scottsville: UKZN Press.

Worden, Nigel (1995) *The Making of Modern South Africa: Conquest, Segregation and Apartheid*. New Jersey, US: Wiley Blackwell.

SCENE 2

Ashwin Singh: Egg or Chicken: A Writer/Director's Recipe in Interviews and Analysis

Deborah A Lutge

"Now the author is dead, and the author is Apartheid."
Zakes Mda (quoted in Naidoo, 1997: 252)

For South African Theatre context has always proved to be a factor intricately woven into our socio-political inheritance. After twenty-six years of democracy, with changed, or with fluctuating notions of what should constitute the 'polis', the enhanced significance of community, as an expression of identity and agency, is evident in the socio-cultural shifts. Aristotle advocated the notion that "man is a political animal" (Rospide & Sorlin, 2015: 30). If this notion is accepted then, man is an essential part of the polis. In a theatrical context it is the writer who acknowledges and highlights these shifts, the director who seeks conceptual context and interpretation, and the participating audience who through discovery are enlightened by contemplating what they assume that they already unconsciously know and what they thought they understood from the new angle or perspective.

In 1994, South Africa underwent, in a single act, the most radical socio-political change of the latter half of the 20th Century. The lines of voters queuing to make their voices heard for the first time bore testimony to this radical swing. Now the South African black voice counted. Much has been said about the impact of protest theatre as a theatre inspiring dynamic movement. Texts, literary and performance, publicised Struggle voices that echoed the call for mass solidarity. Advocacy included the mobilisation of a populace roused by songs and cries for freedom, as theatrical content contradicted white propaganda. Denialism was questioned more frequently in white theatre going circles. Segal claims Western audiences who had turned a blind eye to racial injustice, renegotiated their former global denial after the 1964 Rivonia Trials. (1964: 394-5). In South Africa, status quo options that expected segregated audiences, were no longer perceived as logical, and simply not tolerated by independence in 1994 (Johnson, 1994). Theatre is no longer just a question of preaching to the politically converted but an irrevocable distancing from historical cultural enclaves. More adventurous audiences engaged in a honeymoon period as long as it meant attending the theatre in their region. This is not to deny that even with the integration of audiences, the denialism of many audience members attending the 'close your eyes and think of England' theatre into the 90s and beyond persisted as an escape from the diabolical economic divisions evident, as theatre continued to be divided along cultural lines by choice rather than prescription.

The insinuation of locale in the reference to Durban and the communal portrait of being 'Indian in Durban' in the title of Singh's anthology, signify cultural exclusivity too. Therefore, it is noteworthy that in the production of these Singh plays, the constant intracultural interrelationship of writer, directors, and audiences exerted a cross-cultural appeal. South Africans related to Singh's sardonic critique on South African socio-politics, his observation of character through dialogic subliminal messaging, and his kaleidoscopic interpretation of regional interrelationships. Sometimes in Singh's work what is not said is as powerful as what is said. The discussion between Sibusiso and Kajol in *To House* inscribes the notion of the shifting parameters of the extended 'Indian' family when Kajol says in relation to 'circulating' her mother between family members: "This is what Indians are becoming." (H 48). Kajol reflects on the varied gender expectations in her discussion of her brother touring while she herself retains the role of the duty-bound daughter (H 48). Sibusiso suggests an old age home and Kajol recognizes the suggestion as an attempt to avoid responsibility, calling this action "the white thing to do" (H 48). The inference is that white colonials remain in denial, refusing to acknowledge their responsibility in the apartheid debacle, while abdicating all guilt in the colonial privilege experienced. Kajol insinuates her sense of responsibility to her mother and Sibusiso attempts to dissuade Kajol from proposing her mother move in with the couple, by playing the race card: "Hey I can take care of myself. (*Awkward pause.*) You think your mother is going to live with a black man?" (H 49). Difference is attributed to culture, to race, and to the degree of struggle and success and Sibusiso confirms his acceptance as impacted by the polite gentility of Kajol's mother and his successful position as a lawyer (H 49). Culture, race and socio-economic class are inextricably bound.

As South Africans contemplate the reimagining of the participating roles between writer, director and audience, the socio-political links are again clearly visible. The pandemic has radically changed the logistics and operation of live performance and may indeed change the method of delivery, yet the constant interdependence of writer, director, and audience continues as an abacus awaiting the reinterpretation in a changed socio-political context. Notwithstanding global changes, a shift does not negate a past - it grows out of it. Society's constant companion is flux, a fluidity complicating the tracing of 'roots'. This is not limited to South Africa or to the South African diaspora but flux is a common feature resulting in a complex interweaving of world dynamics. The complexities of understanding 'our present', requires underpinning our understanding by identifying root causes, for the underbelly of the collective has consequences that determine future accountability. The vulnerable and the weak will determine on what future society will make pronouncements. Further, future accountability is dependent on our acknowledgement of past displacement, marginalisation and migration, on what is justified, what is hidden, and what condemned. Past rather than present reception provides the catalyst for the manner in which social inequities are internalized. Our accountability in the future presupposes an assumption of the way we experience consequences from the past, rather than on an engagement with the past, since the present is attempting to move forward. Socially internalized injustices do not die, they emerge therapeutically through the guidance provided by writers or playwrights attempting to conscientise community or society at large. This experiential trajectory configures texts differently and differentiates written text from performance text and from textual reception. But what if the creator and interpreter are the same person? If so, how does this make a notable difference? In a theatrical context does the directorial eye transliterate the writing during the creative phase or does the finished text firmly entrench directorial concepts derived from a familiarity with the creative writing process? Is the finished product then crafted by writer or director? Is this a linear or a spherical construct?

A dialectical answer (that of Hegel and Marx) is that the egg and chicken exist in a dialectical relationship; the problem according to this answer, is that we are approaching an organic/dialectical relationship with the mindset of formal logic, i.e. linear cause-and-effect. Using this mindset, we reach a paradox, for we only see it in terms of 'this caused that.' To reach the true nature of this relationship, we have to admit the fact that the egg creates the chicken just as much as the chicken creates the egg (Hodgson, 1986: 219). But playscripts are distinctive from other forms of creative writing for without this kind of text the director of script-based works has no blueprint and without the director or an astute reader, the playwright's script remains a blueprint without a building.

Looking at the 21st Century

In Joseph Heller's 1961 novel the character Yossarian, in attempting to avoid flight, requires proof of insanity, which if produced would conversely prove sanity. Catch-22 inscribes our history, as well as our quest to contextualise our existence, just as it inscribed the Aristotelian premise. Aristotle too grappled with the notion of roots. He argued that if the first human had been born without father or mother – it would have contradicted natural order as a first egg presupposes a first bird, and a bird comes from an egg (Waller, 1998: 851-853).

The relationship between playwright and director is so interwoven that it reminds me very much of the egg-chicken conundrum: for without a play the director cannot direct, and without a director the play's function is incomplete. This paradoxical notion applies broadly to our attempts to deconstruct the social milieu. The scales in our argument are evenly balanced between our logical conceptualising of individual identity on the one hand, and cultural roots on the other. The individual is distinct from cultural roots, yet inscribed with a specific socio-cultural identity. Therefore, there is this quest to uncover a past that explains the meaning of present existence, in order to direct our individual future efforts, is inherent in our humanity; our identity; our agency; our roots; and our sense of *Ubuntu*. It is this that makes us essentially human and characters are informed by these identifiable behavioural patterns in South African theatre.

The COVID-19 global lockdown may shift historical sourcing and the shifts in theatre will grow out of how artists understood this shift contextualised within historical frameworks. Frequently, as in Mda's syllogism, authors source living material in the graves of the past. The oxymoron of South African Theatre currently lies in the notion of paradoxical poles: what might be termed a 'struggling-free-market-system'; a democracy in search of freedom; an espousing of 'equity' and basic constitutional human rights, in a country with dysfunctional service delivery. Hence our preoccupation with history remains the vehicle of current theatre, and the same is true for Ashwin Singh's anthology *Durban Dialogues, Indian Voice*.

Arguably the shifts in the 21st Century have already signalled a departure, a migration, not only from the 20th Century mind-set, encouraged by global communication on a world-wide web, but through the transmigration of worldviews, further reconfigured by border crossings and world-wide cultural melting-pots. Wars and the refugee displacement of diverse populaces disempowers the impact of borders, evident in the 2016 migratory mapping of refugees across Europe[1] as the war against COVID-19 re-entrenches borders, military presence, fear and isolation and while the economically disempowered suffer most.

Contributing factors are attributed to the constantly widening economic disjuncture between the 'haves' and the 'have nots'. In purportedly 'post-colonial' environments, this contemporary social fissure appears vested across race, gender, sexuality, religious persuasion and ethnicity. Frequently mobility lies in the individual's post-colonial quest to reinvent narrative, agency and voice. Hence the particular relevance of Ashwin Singh's themes in this anthology. *To House* focuses on socio-economic mobility (23-70). There is a preoccupation with Islamic terrorism in the face of impending internal South African revolution in *Duped* (71-116). The internal strife threatened by current rising unemployment alludes to an almost prophetic prediction as we learn of current looting of trucks and shops during the South African lockdown. Corporate take-overs control the conclusion in *Spice'n Stuff* (117-162) and this too is echoed as we watch small businesses being swallowed up by corporate giants lucrative enough to survive a pandemic and online shopping being prioritised this year. In *Reoca Light*, the demise of the African dream is evident (163-186), and remains on our trajectory as we face the onset of a global economic depression post-COVID-19. Finally, the consequences of changing landscapes for women and the effects of a helplessly flailing education are covered in *Beyond the Big Bangs* (187-220). Even in this final

---

1   www.bbc.com/news/world-europe-34175795 [Accessed: 14 June 2019]

astute acknowledgement the reverberations are real with education resorting to remote learning in South Africa and an estimated 66% unable to access the learning distance channels provided, therefore confirming that although influenced by society, playwrights in reflection influence society allowing communities to grapple with new complexities.

South African Thematic Shifts

Each theme in Singh's work is counterpoised against an understanding of pre-conditions in South Africa. Racial restrictions in terms of area, employment, and relationships are explored in *To House* (H 23-70). The revolutionary redefinition of hegemony, broached in *Duped*, assumes comparative analogies with a quasi-Nazi heritage (D 71-116). The demise of 'corner shop' individuality and crafted uniqueness, in favour of the emergence of business giants and monopolies in *Spice 'n Stuff*, signify a corporate control powerful enough to squeeze out the smaller fish, thereby continuing the disenfranchisement of the past (SS 17-162). Past hopes of indentured Indians are juxtaposed against the ingrained violence, the bitter guilt and regrets and the disempowering suspicions and conditions left behind by an aggressive apartheid regime in *Reoca Light* (RL 163-186). The intra-cultural fusion and dislocation of roots indicates urban dissatisfaction that prompts suburban relocation in *Beyond the Big Bangs* (BBB 187-220).

Singh as playwright flexes the irony of each moment, with dialogue laced in sardonic humour. Here business and ownership of the economy is fronted in Deena's exit line in scene 11 which stings while ringing at Jason's ineptitude: "Let's see if you can construct a strategic projection, like a manager would" (H 64) or Sibusiso's accusation that acknowledges Jason as a fired thief: "Ah shame. You brought in so much money you had to steal some" (H 69) and the later play on this when Jason accuses Sibusiso of stealing [whites'] jobs and Sibusiso's response: "Steal[ing] our jobs. In the company from which you stole? … You're used to a certain lifestyle" (H 69). Archetypal characters allow readers, actors, directors and audience to easily recognise peripheral phenomena. In reading the anthology as a literary text we conclude that the social movement that prompts the reconstruction of identity and community, re-inscribes the negotiations of race, culture and gender. Reverting to the legacy of assimilation and colonial-styled hegemony allows us to glance beyond the stereotypical caricature and intended cliché, as perception takes us back to the character as political, or inscribed by the 'polis' environment. Thus, through evaluating the nostalgic dream as well as the realities of 'being African', the plays confront us with the license of freedom. Singh acknowledges that as South Africans we are attempting to renegotiate boundaries and borders previously legally entrenched. His critique notes that the constitution is central to dismantling the fascist legal system, but has this left everyone unprotected? The fences do not come down. The walls are built higher, and protection remains the domain of the wealthy. In South Africa - the 20th Century embodied by segregation, intolerance and alienation - was perceived as globally, nationally and locally dysfunctional. Hence the need for reflection. Ashwin Singh's anthology of five works, *Durban Dialogues, Indian Voices* is a 21st Century reaction to the incumbent complications inherent in this dysfunction as well as the world beyond.

In place of the entrenched national frontiers of the 20th Century, the 21st Century proposes the break-down of narrow definitions of culture, religion, gender and sexual orientation without preparing for the inherent complications. Towards the close of the 20th Century, restrictions were internally deconstructed prompted by the freedom communicated across internet. Movements defied confinement, and enlightenment embraced global inclusivity - as distinct from global assimilation, so what went wrong? Acclaimed South African playwright Mike van Graan, in response to what needs to be communicated in contemporary society and the potential global analogies, answers:

> We are a society in transition, with all the tensions, anxieties, hopes and possibilities attached to that. Our theatre, art and literature – in my view – need to be exploring these, helping us through this transition. We live in a globalised world, impacted upon and impacting on the world around us, so that our theatre also needs to be interrogating … exposing the relationship/s between the individual and the collective, the micro and the macro, the national and the international through human stories. I'm not sure what constitutes a 'global' voice, as theatre needs to be doing this for its individual, specific contexts and should this resonate with situations elsewhere, this becomes global. (Lutge, 2016c)

The transmigration and the shutdown of the 21st Century goes further taking the internal re-evaluation of identity across physical facades, confronting the masks, and questioning the ethos of change in a world of economic re-alignments. Frontier crossings, border closures, socio-economic disparities, diffusing cultural enclaves all predetermine the future effects of marginalisation, memory, historical reading and contemporary context. The past provides a confused mapping of prevailing conditions that evidence an allusion to contemporary concomitant shifts. This raises questions centred on the sphere of influence of 21st Century writers and directors as the canvas for writers and directors moves to embrace the internationalisation of texts: literary and performance. Malika Ndlovu sees "… the local and specific as the primary creative site from which universal relevance and resonance emerges" (Lutge, 2016b); Shantal Singh seeks the authentic South African voices exploring "an evolving, democratic society … rich in cultural tapestry". Singh bemoans the "over-proliferation of Eurocentric work" connoting foreign values as well as the divisiveness of language materialising as inhibitors of "dialogue driven" theatre.

She further asserts that: "We clearly need to communicate with each other … [as] theatre should be seen as the window to our souls" (Lutge, 2016e).

Es'kia Mphahlele in *The Tyranny of Place and Aesthetics* talks to the "inhibiting effects" that the separation from South Africa had on constructing the Struggle writer's literary landscape (Naidoo, 1997: 251). Mphahlele notes the trauma of grappling with African identity, while in exile. Mda too, notes democracy as the dirge for some playwrights and storytellers, reliant on political activism, social realism, and documenting historical hegemonies in order to conscientise audiences, through socio-cultural awareness. Conversely Zakes Mda in an interview with Venu Naidoo for *Alter*nation, argues for the imaginative process and the global influences garnered in reading widely from Gibson Kente and Wole Soyinka to Joe Orton or Harold Pinter. He concurs that there are elements of absurdism as well as postcolonial magic realism in *his* work. Mda avers that in confronting so called "objective reality" he wrote about "the world that I created". He explains: "I am in the God business. I am the God of that world, so I can make things happen the way I want them to happen" (Naidoo, 1997: 250).

The Anthology in Context

The paradigms, as evidenced above, dictate an eclecticism infused with transnational narratives, intracultural fusion-styled structure, and a perspective advocated by the contemplation of the disjuncture between diaspora (migration) and milieu (environment), and the seemingly controversial effects of COVID-19 on communities unable to socially distance due to informal settlements and their dismal living conditions. This reflects Singh's prophetic writings and is the stuff of Ashwin Singh's *Durban Dialogues, Indian Voices*. Further in Singh's writings there is a search for identity, for 'I-content' - a term, not located in notions of *Ubuntu* - but coined for this chapter to agglomerate the 'I' as in 'me' and the digital attempt to cater to our demand for immediacy, entitlement and the ability to access personal freedom as well as the changing continuums perceived in pandemic isolation as well as in *To House*. These traits of entitlement are visible in the closing moments of the play during Sibusiso's accusation of the social façade, of keeping up appearances by shopping at exclusive malls because: "Taking money from a big firm is okay. It's the way you were brought up. You were always given everything … You had an economic system designed to make you rich." (H 70). The repetition of greed is compounded further through Sibusiso's final acknowledgement that his aspirations extend to encompassing everyone else's goals as body corporate chairman, senior lecturer, expert on informal settlements invited to speak to issues on national television, and world famous personality reclaiming the world Jason lost (H 70). (see Conquergood, 2002: 145, citing Gilroy, 1994; Appadurai, 1996; Lavie

& Swedenburg, 1996; Cliffard, 1997; di Leonardo, 1998; Joseph, 1999; Ong, 1999; and Taylor, 1999).

I contend that this ownership of the uniquely conflicted South African world, evident in Singh's writings, is because it is a world of trauma in which the stakes are raised through excessive levels of violence, anger and guilt. This search for transparency, this quest to reposition 'other', this profundity inscribed in positioning humanity as teetering amidst the smoke on the edge of survival, raises the stakes and makes social pulses surge. The post-apartheid anti-climax, suggests drained intensity, and the junkie's nervous malaise or a numbed indifference – perhaps the kind that writers in exile seem to have experienced. Could this sense of loss, this loss of contact account for activists such as Mphahlele sensing a disengagement with their African identity? How does this contention align with Mda's concerns that writers are creating less with the easier lifestyle of democracy? Is this the reason that current activists, who interrogate the effects of the past on democracy, have not lost their creative impulse? Ashwin Singh alleges that

> issues … prevalent in our local communities … inevitably have universal significance because people all over the world have so many common experiences, challenges, triumphs and tragedies. Theatre … is far less corporate than film and therefore should provide the opportunity to create memorable works of art … I believe we have a particular responsibility in contemporary South Africa to tell local stories and to prioritise these … Apartheid obliterated Black culture in all its forms…it considered our art and other cultural expressions second rate … so we have to expose this lie with more vigour and passion. We truly need an African Cultural Revolution. (Lutge, 2016a)

In Singh's work the continual realigning of perspectives, predetermined by the reader or viewer's new discoveries, is invited through the conflict endorsed by what might be termed the interaction of sacrosanct socio-cultural and political enclaves and the irony invoked in shifting local, national and global assimilation policies. The juxtaposition forces a confrontation of who, what, where, when, and why it is necessary to express ourselves as reinvented humans. The image in motion reflecting back from the sky on the specks that are us in *Duped* moves us to re-interrogate notions of the ever-widening gaps. Reconciliatory *Ubuntu* attempting to redefine social mores amidst the widening economic chasm smacks of fantasy.

The writer, the director, and the audience in South Africa inevitably encompass linguistic, socio-cultural, spiritual, political, racial and gender diversity straddling pasts filled with racial prescriptiveness, distinctive socio-economic experience, and vastly divergent political landscapes that are evident now, during lockdown, more than ever before. Director Ralph Lawson contends that: "we are a magnificently polyglot society, and our stories need to reflect this. I would say that this is the feature which mainly sets us apart from global voices" (Lutge, 2016d).

So if the writer belongs to one diverse grouping how is this negotiated in the conceptual translation from literary to performance text? Mike van Graan notes significantly how collaboration impacts product: "Casting is probably the key element in how one's text is viewed. The more technically skilled, experienced and 'branded' the actors (and director), the better the text is interpreted and presented" (Lutge, 2016c).

Sociocultural and Political Constructs

By implication, therefore, the theatrical archetype itself supersedes socio-cultural and political constructs, albeit that the choice to collaborate may indeed be influenced by common criteria within the polyglot society or the method of delivery. Therefore, notwithstanding the diverse influences and contexts, the transmigration that occurred in protest theatre collaborations, notably: Kani, Ntshona and Fugard's theatre; Purkey's Junction Theatre plays; or Ngema, Mtwa, and Simon's works; intracultural reflection is evident in Singh's contemporary writer and director collaborations mounted by a series of directors from racially and culturally diverse backgrounds. The directors included among others: Themi Venturas directing *Spice 'n Stuff* at the Playhouse Loft (2010) and at the Sandton Theatre on the Square (2011); Ralph Lawson directing *Reoca Light* at the Loft (2017); *To House* in the Drama (2017) and *Into the Grey* in the Loft (2018) at the Durban Playhouse Complex and *Reoca Light* (2019) at the Tara Theatre in London; Edmund Mhlongo directing *Culture Clash* (2013) at the Loft; Caroline Smart directing *To House* at the Playhouse (2006) and *Spice 'n Stuff* at the Catalina Theatre (2007); Debbie Lutge directing *Duped* at the Courtyard Theatre (2017); as well as the writer himself directing *Beyond the Big Bangs* (2016). Inscribed in Singh's writing too, is the recognition of a single national imperative in order to reconnect across social divides, as well as to extend across borders in line with internationalisation trends. This signifies globally connecting contexts, by inviting and encompassing multi-layered perspectives, acknowledging the shift away from tunnelled world-views grown in isolation, whether internally or externally constructed. Three centuries of South African Struggle under colonialism provides a paradigm that pre-empts and yet is intricately woven in British Prime Minister Harold Macmillan's 'Wind of Change'[2] parliamentary debate, delivered on 3 February 1960 in Cape Town. So our inevitable South African theatrical syllogism coined by Mda[3] could arguably be reconstituted as 'the past is dead, until memory is the author', providing an authorial catalyst for future global literary direction as Europe faces the 21st Century refugee crisis or the world fights a global pandemic.

---

2   https://www.sahistory.org.za/article/wind-change-speech [Accessed 14 June 2019]
3   "Now the author is dead, and the author is Apartheid" Zakes Mda (quoted in Naidoo, 1997: 252)

The Chicken - Egg Paradox

Both directors and audiences read texts differently as the conscious choices of the director evolved in rehearsal process are frequently only unconsciously experienced as audio-visual stimuli by audiences. Theatre patrons simultaneously interpret - in a single sitting - content as well as directorial framing. Textual writing, reading and reception, influenced by the literary medium versus the production experience, confirm the variance in the literary and performance text debate. Audiences attending Shakespearean productions frequently attempt to battle their way through a literary text that, once mounted or placed in celluloid, enable the form to be read in much the same way as an advert hints subliminally at associated influences. Conversely Amy S. Green in *The Revisionist Stage: American Directors Reinvent the Classics* addresses the supplanting of authorial voice and the emergence of the 'director-author'. Shantal Singh, answering a questionnaire I circulated to selected practitioners, refers back to the 'authenticity' of voice inscribed in the original vision. Yet, once a playwright confers rights, the writer is effectively powerless, if the reinterpretation of text is subject to an erudite directorial interpretation and the production based on empirical observation, critical analysis, and what Conquerwood calls "a distanced perspective" (Conquerwood, 2016: 146). He concurs that propositional knowledge "anchored in paradigm and … print" is thereby juxtaposed against practice anchored in ephemeral context, whether envisioned in the writing or not. Hence the 'chicken or egg' primacy paradox. The creative director strives to resonate between text and audience-expectation and, as Ashwin Singh contends, "realize the action and … emotion … [as well as] ensure a rhythm" (Lutge, 2016a). The relationship between writer and director is a mutually influential one, and it is the critical detachment that is the key to a solid working relationship. Ralph Lawson describes it as "a tricky mix" inscribed with "trust on the part of the writer who surrenders control", followed by confidence in the expertise of a skilled director capable of providing "another eye on the work … and [Lawson asserts] isolation and objectivity can unearth a number of points of which the playwright was perhaps only subconsciously aware" (Lutge, 2016d). In *Theatre Directing in South Africa*, Durban writer-director Neil Coppen claims his theatre apprenticeship left him fascinated by the concept of 'total theatre' where " … visual symbols and elements [are] as seminal as the text … " (quoted in Twijnstra & Durden, 2013: 16). This asserts the need for the writer/director to visualise the potential of the text in motion and, where the writer directs their own work, it is the realisation of this visualised concept that prompts many writers to grapple with the first staging of their untested text. South African theatre-entrepreneur, Greg Homann, holds that theatre in South Africa "is director driven" and "rarely driven by the writer or producer" (quoted in Twijnstra & Durden, 2013: 22-24). As an arts entrepreneur, Homann, inspired by Malcolm Purkey - whom he avows was the director that "conscientized him into the complexity of South Africa [...] almost always finds the projects rather than the project finding him" (quoted in Twijnstra & Durden, 2013: 22-24). Lunacharsky in "Theses on the Problems of Marxist Criticism" contends:

> Our literature is passing through one of the decisive moments in its development. A new life is being built in the country, and literature is learning more and more to reflect this life in its as yet undefined and unstable forms; evidently, too, it can pass to a problem of a still higher order – to the political and, in particular, the moral influence on the very process of construction. (cited in Dukore, 1974: 949)

Having noted many of the paradoxes inherent in this debate, centred on creative hegemony, a further complication derives from the critical detachment of the subject matter embraced in the initialising work of the director. If the writer alone authenticates the voice does this propose limitations for future productions? Or does reinterpretation run the supplementary gauntlet of frequent misinterpretation? Does the writer's careful negotiation of the initial mounting guide future mountings, expectations, or critical reception? In translation, how are bridges forged and is this gap the responsibility of the literary text or the performance text?

> Yes, there is a huge difference between how a text is reviewed as a literary piece on the one hand and as a performance piece on the other. The literary piece stands on its own, and is evaluated as a piece of literature/writing. A performance gives life to the text and the evaluation/reviewing evaluates not just the text, but the performances, the directing, the design, etc – the full, holistic presentation of the theatre piece. This is as it should be. (Lutge 2016c)

Conclusion

In a 21st century post-colonial setting, both director and playwright reinvent the wheel, treat the reconditioning, transform the angles, and merge the historical reflection. Benedetti in *The Director at Work* (1985) distinguishes broadly between the "conservative position", seeking "fidelity" to the text, the "liberal position", striving for "relevance" of the interpretation of the text, and the "radical position", evidencing creativity derived from the text (Benedetti, 1985:13-16). However, this does not mean that these categories necessarily align with literature, although literature would seem to be constructed along three broad lines too: first, traditional lines; second, re-constructed or recontextualised lines, informed by the contemporary socio-cultural or political perspective; third, deconstructed lines that, by drawing on and rereading tradition, deviate or reflect upon the implied messaging and associations (see Silverman, 1989: 2).

As narratives around live theatre are reimagined globally with current theatre closures due to COVID-19, concomitant unemployed artists seeking to reimagine theatrical possibilities under new social distancing auditorium and performance requirements, as well as the regulations governing the imperatives of donning public masks, means distanced audiences impacting already dwindled ticket sales in South Africa. Will this consequent effect on salaries, further prioritise the compacting of the role of writer-directors and solo or minimal cast performances in the immediate future? Certainly it will pose challenges for unestablished writers and directors entering a newly imagined arena where the economics of mounting plays with rising ticket prices and contained fragmented, audiences derives less sponsorship and investment in the youth than needed. The question this raises is one of continuing negotiation.

Albeit the overlapping mapping of rhythmic patterning between writer and director may either converge or diverge, there remains a constant distinction between both the writer and director's processes. The directorial vision lies in the immediacy of the directing process, while the literary text gravitates towards the permanence of the written publication, and yet both are considered process as well as product-driven activities. The result of the chicken/egg textual recipe, is an exposition of our human narratives. Ashwin Singh's concern with embracing this South African voice explores who we are and how we connect in the literary text as well as in the mounted production.

In conclusion, the encapsulation of Ashwin Singh's works, are perhaps best epitomised in this Mahatma Gandhi quote:

> I do not want my home to be walled in on all sides and its windows to be stuffed. I want cultures of all lands to be blown about my house as freely as possible. But I refuse to be blown off my feet by any (quoted in Mehta, 2000: 630).

Bibliography

Appadurai, A. 1996 *Modernity at Large: Cultural Dimensions of Globalization*. Minneapolis: University of Minnesota Press.

Benedetti, R. L. 1985. *The Director at Work*. New Jersey: Prentice Hall.

Bharucha, Rustom. 1993. *Theatre and the World: Performance and the Politics of Culture*. London: Routledge.

Clifford, J. 1997. *Routes: Travel and Translation in the Late Twentieth Century*. London: Harvard University Press.

Conquergood, Dwight. 2002. *Performance Studies: Interventions and Radical Research. TDR/The Drama Review, Vol 46.2, 145-156. Summer 2002*. New York, NY: New York University and the Massachusetts Institute of Technology. https://doi.org/10.1162/105420402320980550

Di Leonardo, Micaela. 1998. *Exotics at Home: Anthropologies, Others, American Modernity*. Chicago: University of Chicago Press.

Dukore, Bernard, F. 1974. *Dramatic Theory and Criticism: The Greeks to Grotowsky*. New York, NY: Rinehart and Winston.

Fénelon, François. 1825. *Abrégé des vies des anciens philosophes*, Paris 1726: 314. Translation: *Lives of the Ancient Philosophers*, London 1825: 202.

Gilroy, Paul. 1994. After the love has gone: Bio-politics and etho-poetics in the black public sphere, *Third Text*, 8 (28-29): 25-46. https://doi.org/10.1080/09528829408576500

Govinden, D.B. 2013. A Critical Overview. Ashwin Singh's *Durban Dialogues, Indian Voice: Five South African Plays*. Twickenham, UK: Aurora Metro Books.

Green, Amy S. 2006. The Revisionist Stage: American Directors Reinvent the Classics. *Cambridge Studies in American Theatre and Drama*. Vol 3, 1-244. reprint New York: Cambridge UP.

Hodgson, Geoff. 1986. Behind methodological individualism, *Cambridge Journal of Economics*, 10 (3) September: 211–224. https://doi.org/10.1093/oxfordjournals.cje.a034996

Johnson, W. R. 1994. Dismantling apartheid: A South African town in transition. *The Anthropology of Contemporary Issues*, August 4. Ithaca: Cornell UP.

Joseph, M. 1999. *Nomadic Identities: The Performance of Citizenship*. (First edition ed.). Minneapolis: University of Minnesota Press. muse.jhu.edu/book/32163.

Kholofelo, Sedibe. 1998. Dismantling Apartheid Education: an overview of change. *Cambridge Journal of Education*, 28 (3), November: 269-282. https://doi.org/10.1080/0305764980280302

Lavie, Smadar & Swedenburg, Ted. 1996 Between and among the boundaries of culture: Bridging text and lived experience in the third timespace, *Cultural Studies*, 10 (1): 154-179, https://doi.org/10.1080/09502389600490501

Lee, I. C., Pratto, F., & Johnson, B. T. 2011. Intergroup consensus/disagreement in support of group-based hierarchy: an examination of socio-structural and psycho-cultural factors. *Psychological Bulletin*, 137(6), 1029–1064. https://doi,org/10.1037/a0025410

Mehta, P, B. 2000. "Cosmopolitanism and the Circle of Reason". *Political Theory*, 28 (5), October: 619-639. Sage Publications, Inc. Stable, http://www.jstor.org/stable/192291_

Migrant crisis: What next for Germany's asylum seekers? - Section Europe. 2015. *BBC World News*. 14 September. http://www.bbc.com/news/world-europe-34175795_

Mulgan, R.G. 1974. Aristotle's Doctrine That Man Is a Political Animal. *Hermes*, 102. Bd., H.3, Franz Steiner Verlag: 438-445. http://www.jstor.org

Naidoo, Venu. 1997. Interview: Interview with Zakes Mda. *Alternation*, 4(1): 247-261.

Ong, A. 1999. *Flexible Citizenship: The Cultural Logic of Transnationality*. Durham: Duke UP.

Rospide, Maylis and Sandrine Sorlin. 2015. *The Ethics and Poetics of Alterity: New Perspectives on Genre Literature*. Newcastle upon Tyne: Cambridge Scholars Publishing.

Segal, R 1964. *Sanctions Against South Africa*. Harmondsworth: Penguin.

Silverman, D. 1993, 2001, 2006. *Interpreting Qualitative Data: Methods for analysing Talk, Text and Interaction. Ed. 3*. London: SAGE Publications

Singh, A. 2013. *Durban Dialogues, Indian Voice: Five South African Plays*. An Anthology. UK: Aurora Metro Books.

Simons, J. 1997. Drama Pedagogy and the Art of Double Meaning. *Research in Drama Education: The Journal of Applied Theatre and Performance*, 2 (2): 193-201. Published online: 07 Jul 2006. https://doi.org/10.1080/1356978970020205

Taylor, C. 1999. Democratic exclusion (and its remedies?). In: A Cairns, J. Courtney, P. MacKinnon, J. Michelmann, and D Smith (eds). *Citizenship, diversity, and pluralism: Canadian & Comparative Perspectives*. Montreal: McGill-Queen's University Press, 265-287.

Twijnstra, Roel & Emma Durden. 2014. *Theatre Directing in South Africa: Skills and Inspirations*. SA: Jacana Media

Waller, D. 1998. The Chicken and Her Egg. *Mind*, 107 (428): 851-853. www.jstor.org/stable/2659791

Emails:

Lutge, D. A. 2016a. Unpublished Interview with Ashwin Singh. Generated on email on: 7 May 2016.

Lutge, D. A. 2016b. Unpublished Interview with Malika Ndlovu. Generated on email on: 27 May 2016

Lutge, D. A. 2016c. Unpublished Interview with Mike van Graan. Generated on email on: 27 May 2016

Lutge, D. A. 2016d. Unpublished Interview with Ralph Lawson. Generated on email on: 27 May 2016

Lutge, D. A. 2016e. Unpublished Interview with Shantal Singh. Generated on email on: 27 May 2016

Lutge, D. A. 2016f. Unpublished Interview with Steven Stead. Generated on email on: 27 May 2016

Lutge, D. A. 2016g. Unpublished Interview with Themi Venturas. Generated on email on: 27 May 2016.

SCENE 3

From Rockets to Robots: The Function of Science Fiction Icons in Ashwin Singh's *Duped*

J. Coplen Rose

Introduction[1]

In 2018 the National Arts Festival in Makhanda, South Africa, featured a performance written and directed by Johann Smith titled *Gods of My Country*. The production, presented by Theatrerocket, satirically responded to political scandals and national crises affecting South Africans. In one salient moment, a character makes a pitch to a panel of entertainment industry executives for the next blockbuster by describing the logic and structure of apartheid as a possible plotline. Satire occurs when the executives reject the proposal on the basis that they do not want to produce a work of science fiction, or SF. For the panel, South Africa's recent past sounds so surreal that it must be a work of fiction. The incongruity of this moment required audience members to reconcile the slippage between a genre associated with alien landscapes and strange encounters to a known historical reality. In doing so the 2018 performance in Makhanda encouraged its audience to view the nation and its history from a different angle, considering how apartheid might be classified as SF by someone unfamiliar with the nation's past.

Gods of My Country is by no means the first South African performance to foreground links between apartheid and concepts associated with SF. This tradition can be traced back at least as early as the nineteen-seventies with Credo Mutwa's *uNosilimela* (1973) and Pieter-Dirk Uys's *God's Forgotten* (1975). However, recent references to SF indicate this genre continues to support critical responses to national crises. As the example from *Gods of My Country* illustrates, SF can encourage people to view the nation and its history in new ways. Approaching this joke from another angle, such humour also highlights the dangers of discounting SF as imaginative, and therefore of no interest to a national body confronting serious challenges beyond independence. Paraphrasing John Rider's *Colonialism and the Emergence of Science Fiction*, James H. Thrall's statement that it "is something of a truism that colonial themes have permeated science fiction from its earliest years" suggests otherwise (2009). The intersection between imperialism and SF may serve as an important

---

1 I wish to thank the Acadia University Research Fund for generously supporting this project

site for intervention, a space where South African playwrights can challenge apartheid discourses in order to rethink post-independence nationalism.

Science Fiction and Ashwin Singh's *Duped*

Similar to *Gods of My Country*, Ashwin Singh's *Duped* (2011) mixes satire and SF to explore apartheid's traumatic legacy. In doing so, Singh's play epitomises Ericka Hoagland and Reema Sarwal's assertion that SF is often "a forward looking project that is frequently rooted in anxieties about the present (as well as the past)" (2010:9). In *Duped*, these anxieties manifest through characters' relationships to technology. Rather than making life easier, technology frequently alienates characters from one another or causes them to confront hard realities around social and political divisions in Durban. Although technology is ubiquitous in the play, Singh uses three prominent SF icons to explore national crises in the post-apartheid period: a spaceship, an android, and computer chip technology capable of mind control. By situating his audience in the future through SF icons, Singh maps how apartheid power structures continue to shape people's personal relationships, use of space, and national unity. Importantly, Singh uses SF icons to present current anxieties about the nation's future as part of a linear arc originating in the state's traumatic past. *Duped* concludes by warning its audience that the distrust and self-interest dividing South Africans can be exploited to establish neo-imperial systems of control.

Discussing the role of icons in SF, Gwyneth Jones posits they "are the signs which announce the genre, which warn the reader that this is a different world; and at the same time constitute that difference" (2003:163). Icons should be recognisable and overt in their signalling of a different society with its own set of codes. For Jones, the construction of an alternate world is the defining attribute of the genre, a "feature that unites every kind of sf" (2003:163). Icons are not only crucial in foregrounding an alternate reality, their alterity adheres to specific conventions. Jones explains this by tracing the etymology of the term icon back to Byzantine art where "ikons" are stylised portrayals of saints and Jesus Christ (2003:163). Merging this concept with SF conventions, she outlines the three guiding principles of an icon: they signify something "other-worldly" or "supernatural," they are "artistically conventional," and yet they also "clearly belong to the public domain" (2003:163). So, while icons tend to possess compulsory attributes, they are also widely adapted and modified by writers so that "it is probably fruitless to trace any of the icons of sf back to a single, original author" (Jones, 2003:163). For Jones, the unique modifications that each author makes produce a "variant iconography (a differently designed robot, an idiosyncratic form of faster-than-light drive), to match the writer's particular intention" (2003:163-4). In this sense, studying the adjustments Singh makes to his SF icons can help us better understand the social and political critiques he undertakes in *Duped*.

Singh's play is set in Durban but is temporally situated in a near-future South Africa. The plot revolves around the experiences of Captain Sandra Snyman and Lieutenant Sizwe Khumalo, commanding officers on South Africa's new airship. The vessel, the Airship Equity, hovers invisibly above Durban and is on a mission to uncover a terrorist plot connected to an international conference. With only a few days to solve the case, the crew is working with limited knowledge to locate an Islamic terrorist cell planning to attack visiting delegates. Contributing to this crisis, a junior politician named Julio Masimola joins the mission for the sake of political advancement. While he is not authorised to handle sensitive information, Masimola frequently reveals he has more information than his commanding officers. As this is the first deployment of the airship, the crew also has its American creator, Dr. David Johnson, aboard to ensure the mission goes smoothly. While all characters appear to work towards the same goal, that of maintaining social equilibrium in Durban, secrecy and self-interest fragment the crew. *Duped* concludes by revealing the terrorist plot was a ruse orchestrated by Johnson. His plan to steal the airship is ruined by the arrival of American forces. *Duped* ends with Johnson being arrested and South Africa agreeing to help America in a global war on terrorism in exchange for the return of their airship.

While *Duped* is one of Singh's older plays, it is also one of his lesser-known creations. In recent correspondence he attributes the lack of critical interest in the work to its "mixed-genre style and the science fiction elements" it contains (2019). Although *Durban Dialogues, Indian Voice* identifies its inception as 2011, its synthesis occurred earlier (2013:11). A preliminary version appeared at the 2005 Performing Arts Network of Southern Africa's (PANSA) Playreading Festival. Directed by Megan Furniss, the staged reading was held at the University of Cape Town and Singh performed one of the parts (Singh, 2019). *Duped* was the only finalist from KwaZulu-Natal at this event, a detail which, as Adrienne Sichel's review laments, "says a lot about the ravages of commercialisation on serious theatre in this region" (2005:10). The only complete staging of *Duped* occurred at the Durban University of Technology's Digifest arts festival on 11 November 2017. The production blended performance with multimedia elements, "integrating theatre, film, and virtual reality [in] attempts to push boundaries," as the production's Director, Debbie Lutge, explains (2017). This protracted history means the play reflects upon a range of national crises. However, its brief performance run also means limited scholarship exists on the play.

In terms of timing, its genesis in the early years of the new millennium is significant because it coincides with a major shift in South African theatre. As Greg Homann explains, by "the turn of the millennium there had been a change; theatre-makers were finally confronting contemporary issues rather than rehashing past preoccupations" (2009:11). As citizens grew increasingly sceptical about the achievements related to the nation's transition from apartheid to a democratic state, theatre responded by exploring unresolved divisions and raising serious questions about social and political conditions. Similar to Homann, Marcia Blumberg posits South African theatre after apartheid's dissolution went through two phases: "an initial period of euphoria, patience, and hope; then, the past decade, which has been a 'second interregnum' in South African politics" (2009). For Blumberg, theatre beyond the year 2000 reflects "the instability of conditions" and epitomises a "desperation to break silences" (2009). Singh's handling of topics such as American neo-imperialism, scepticism about national projects of reconciliation, and the dangers corruption poses to economic and geographical redistribution suggest the play is part of the new wave of theatre Blumberg describes erupting a decade after the advent of democracy.

The timing of the play also coincides with a major shift in contemporary SF. As Eric D. Smith explains, the period following the year 2000 witnessed "the phenomenal efflorescence of narratives written within a speculative framework that radically reconfigure the conceptual machinery of SF and utopia to address the exigencies of postcoloniality and globalization" (2012:5). *Duped*, like Lauren Beukes' award-winning cyberpunk novel *Zoo City* (2010) and Neill Blomkamp's *District 9* (2009), is part of the movement of artists using SF to explore postcolonial conditions. Notably, the production of postcolonial SF, a subgenre Andy Sawyer defines as exploring "the nature of Otherness and Futurity, and what happens when these ideas are expressed by those who were the *subjects* of earlier versions [of SF]," was also occurring outside of South Africa (2010:2). Smith locates Nalo Hopkinson and Uppinder Mehan's *So Long Been Dreaming: Postcolonial Science Fiction* (2004) as a catalyst in this new tradition (2012:5). Singh's satire constitutes the kind of reconfiguration that Smith describes because the tools of domination have been stolen from imperial powers, via Johnson's theft of airship technology from America (D 111), and given to victims of domination, specifically those who suffered under apartheid. In doing so, *Duped* uses SF icons to negotiate past trauma and discuss fears people have towards policing, technology, and the dangers South Africa faces in global trade systems.

The Spaceship

Jones's article articulates the difference between rockets and spaceships so as to identify the unique roles these icons inhabit in conventional SF. In the former instance, she notes the rocket's phallic resemblance, its original use as a weapon on medieval Chinese battlefields, and its function as a "symbol of energy and escape" (2003:164). In contrast to the rocket's phallic shape and direct association with weaponry, the spaceship is more often associated with voyage. "Designed not for experimental parabolas but for exploration," Jones explains, "the spaceship (whether it carries colonists or invaders, or hides monsters in its secret depths) is an alternative, contained world in itself" (2003:164). Jones's assertion that the spaceship serves as a limited world reflects one of the three roles the airship occupies in *Duped*. The spaceship itself serves as a microcosm of the state, a vessel which confronts crises similar to those affecting the nation. However, as a mode of transportation, the spaceship also operates as a tool for exploration. Lastly, *Duped* builds on this second attribute to emphasise how narratives of voyage and surveillance parallel imperial processes of control, especially through spatial relationships and visual power structures. This gives rise to the ship's third configuration, as a weapon.

The Spaceship as a Microcosm of the State

The airship's name and the diversity of its crew are allusions to rainbow nationalism. Snyman, a woman of mixed-race ethnicity, works closely with Khumalo, a Zulu, Bobby, an android programmed to sound like a Indian South African, and Johnson, an American who migrated to South Africa. As a microcosm of the state, the crew's diversity reflects the unity and inclusivity conveyed through terminology like Rainbow Nation, a symbol used by leaders such as Nelson Mandela and Archbishop Desmond Tutu to redefine South African nationalism beyond apartheid. As Meg Samuelson explains, "The transition [from apartheid to a democracy] heralded a shift away from a nation characterised by division to one united under the heavy glow of the 'rainbow'" (2007:2). Naming the vessel Airship Equity, Singh begins *Duped* in a manner that places this national metaphor under scrutiny.

Advancing this mode of critique, characters frequently connect the airship project with the country's new spirit. Khumalo, for instance, argues his return to South Africa is proof he "still believe[s] in the dream … a new nation to inspire Africa" (D 78). While Snyman is sceptical of Khumalo's intentions at this point, she accepts his explanation that serving on the airship can help "make a difference" in the new state (D 77). In Khumalo's view the airship, much like the rainbow metaphor, is a model to inspire people. Khumalo reveals this idealism when convincing Snyman not to resign because "too many people are walking away" (D 115). The logic of this argument indicates he sees the ship as a form of technopolitical project, a device which, to employ Paul Edwards and Gabrielle Hecht's definition, entangles "technology with narratives of national and social identity" and which has "concrete political and material outcomes" (2010). In this sense, the Airship Equity embodies the dream of a modern and unified South Africa. Khumalo's view is similarly held by his uncle, the Deputy President, who emphasises the overlap between technology and the nation's spirit when describing the vessel as "South Africa's soul" (D 113). In this regard the ship functions as an allegory as the crises the vessel faces parallel those of the state.

As a national allegory, the array of problems the airship faces reveal the Rainbow Nation is not working. Devarakshanam Betty Govinden discusses Singh's critique of rainbow nationalism throughout *Durban Dialogues, Indian Voice* by commenting that the collection of plays "contribute to the deepening of our democracy in that they prompt a critique of many emerging issues in the present time as we ask: *whither the rainbow nation?*" (2013:13). The critique Govinden discusses extends to Singh's spaceship icon. The airship, like South Africa's transition from apartheid to democracy, is a complex mechanism that its officers are still learning to operate. As there are no instruction manuals to follow in either case, errors are inevitable. Some mistakes aboard the airship are mundane and embarrassing, such as Khumalo accidentally activating the intercom while discussing his disaffection at the "orgy of greed" that has hijacked politicians like Masimola (D 78). However, others such as Khumalo's misplaced trust in Luke Jedison, his half-brother, are serious; Jedison's attempt to steal the airship reveals family bonds can be broken by citizens disenfranchised with national conditions (D 106).

As an enclosed environment, the spaceship is an excellent device to foreground personal divisions. For Jones, "[w]hatever shape the vessel takes it will be the locus for a drama of human relationships, an examination of the ideas of conflict and dependence" (2003:165). As such, the spaceship signifies the opposite of "the rocket's promise of escape from our origins" (Jones, 2003:165). In *Duped*, the spaceship both serves as a self-contained entity, yet it is also vulnerable to national crises. For example, labour protests on Durban's streets spread to the ship when an illegal strike from the Dumisani Domestic Training Union breaks out (D 99). In another instance, Khumalo wonders if an unexpected blackout is load shedding (D 109). The limited space of the vessel amplifies crises because, as a smaller version of the state which is operating on a limited timeline, disruptions are felt immediately.

For instance, the Dumisani Domestic Training Union's illegal strike severely affects its functionality, necessitating a swift resolution. Moreover, this conflict reveals how past trauma and racial divisions influence current labour debates. For Snyman, the labourers' expectations are too high, bargaining for accommodations such as "tea breaks, cappuccino breaks, smoke breaks, Sangoma breaks" as well as "Royal wedding leave" (D 99). Ruminating on the situation in her captain's personal log, she attributes the breakdown in negotiations to racial prejudices carrying over from apartheid. In her view, the union sees her as a "mixed race madam" who is "not black so I don't know struggle" (D 99). Such views, Snyman believes, eschew the exploitation that her own family historically experienced, her monologue noting that her mother was a domestic labourer but "didn't work in the excellent conditions that they do" (D 99). This conflict illustrates how apartheid racial categories continue to compromise projects meant to foster unity.

The prevalence of racism and class divisions aboard the vessel confirm Blumberg's assertion that, while South Africa has one of the world's most progressive constitutions prohibiting "discrimination with respect to race, class, gender, ethnicity, religion, and sexual orientation, it cannot decree changes in the mindsets of individuals and the dynamics of communities" (2009). Such conflicts play out at personal levels, as in the showdown between Snyman and the Dumisani Domestic Training Union (D 99), Snyman's fight against gender-based abuse from Masimola and Khumalo (D 74, 77), but also competing visions for the redistribution of resources after apartheid, a conflict that divides Khumalo and Masimola. In the latter case, Masimola, a parody of Julius Malema, seeks to accrue power through projects intended to rebalance political leadership after apartheid.[2] Such conflicts confirm the Airship Equity is not, in fact, an equitable space at all.

The mobility of the airship has the added advantage of serving to critique the sense of entitlement some hold in the new dispensation. While Masimola is the opportunist fighting to politically control the ship, others such as Johnson and Jedison are liberals-turned-cynics who plot to steal it for their own ends. Johnson plans to sell the ship to China, whereas Jedison plans to sell it to Russia. In this case both view the airship in a manner consistent with Jones's description of a rocket, a vessel that offers the "promise of escape" (2003:165). What is interesting about Singh's use of a spaceship to critique the liberals' cynicism is that, for Johnson, once escape has been effected, the isolation he envisions reflects conventional attributes of a spaceship. Jones's description of the spaceship "forging its lonely way through a vast inimical ocean" (2003:165) parallels Johnson's dream of the "blue waters of an uncomplicated island," a description lacking any reference to national identity (D 110). His rejection of rainbow nationalism connects with SF conventions in that he dreams of a closed space reflective of a conventional spaceship, rather than the dynamic and hybrid space of the airship. Johnson defends his decision to sell the ship on the basis that he is "servicing the demands of the market," a view predicated upon a hierarchy in which capitalist ventures supersede national needs (D 110). Johnson's plan is the ultimate capitulation of South African nationalism to capitalism and self-interest.

The interplay between the politics of decolonisation and South Africa's post-apartheid entrance into global trade is played out through the allegory of ship as nation. This tension seems to confirm Eric Smith's assertion that, "[b]

---

2   Malema was the leader of the African National Congress Youth League when *Duped* debuted in 2011. Singh's parody exaggerates accusations levelled against Malema at this time. Specifically, Malema caused conflict amongst the African National Congress Tripartite Alliance by proposing the nationalisation of South Africa's mines. The ensuing debate saw increasing tensions between Malema and other organisations in the alliance, including the South African Communist Party. Martin Plaut records this conflict led the South African Communist Party to attack "Malema and his associates for being corrupt politicians whose favours had been bought in exchange for an opulent lifestyle" (2010). In Singh's play Masimola lives a lavish lifestyle, drinking "imported sherry at a five star Ballito hotel" prior to a political rally and travelling around Durban in his personal airship (D 76). Throughout *Duped* Masimola comes across as greedy, selfish, and fixated on political promotion.

orn in the imperialist collision of cultural identities and taking as its formal and thematic substance the spatial dislocations that inhere in the imperial situation, science fiction would seem the ideal instrument with which to engage critically the transition from the postcolonial condition to that of globalization" (2012:4). For Singh, the challenges of decolonisation in South Africa dovetail with threats posed by globalisation and neo-imperialism, instigated by the opening up of South Africa's economy to both legitimate, and illegal, global trade. In *Duped*, the slippage between sanctioned trade and illicit trade is nuanced by the fact that Russia and China are visiting Durban for the BRICS (Brazil, Russia, India, China, and South Africa) conference, an arena where trade deals are struck, yet both delegations plan to illegally purchase the spaceship after it is stolen. Connecting this back to the ship as a microcosm of the nation, *Duped* suggests disenfranchised liberals, men with political power and technological expertise, may try to profit by selling state resources to global trade partners who exploit political instability for their own benefit.

The Spaceship as a Device of Exploration

While personal conflicts fracture the equilibrium onboard the Airship Equity, reflecting divisions in the nation overall, the relationship between the vessel and Durban's landscape is equally unsettling. The spaceship connects back to colonial processes of exploration through its arrival and subsequent role policing the state. The airship, like its predecessor the sailing ship, sits at a distance, surveying Durban from a position that affords it safety and an expansive view. Its separation from Durban means the vessel's crew must, like early European explorers landing on Africa's shores, shuttle between the ship and a distant landscape. In *Duped* the smaller ships are described as "supershuttles" and serve the same purpose as their rowboat predecessors, carried aboard sailing ships to grant access to territories without ports (D 88). As there is no landing pad for the airship in Durban, the supershuttles are the only means to access Durban. In this fashion Singh's spaceship icon resembles the technologies and practices of European imperialism.

Scholars of postcolonial SF have widely documented the similarity between spaceships and imperialism. As Istvan Csicsery-Ronay, Jr. notes, the "dominant sf nations are precisely those that attempted to expand beyond their borders in imperialist projects: Britain, France, Germany, Soviet Russia, Japan, and the US" (2003). Working from this premise, he argues SF icons such as super-weapons, spaceships, and robots, "represent the power tools of imperial subjects, the transformations of the objects of domination, and the ambiguities of subjects who find themselves with split affinities" (2003). Spaceships, as vehicles of exploration, frequently produce situations reminiscent of colonial contact with other cultures. Hopkinson exemplifies the violence inherent in this convention by arguing SF memes such as exploring new territories and colonising inhabitants are "not a thrilling adventure story" for the formerly-colonised, "it's non-fiction, and we are on the wrong side of the strange-looking ship that appears out of nowhere" (2004:7). Singh's decision to place South Africans at the helm of the airship reworks this meme.

One of the ways *Duped* modifies such narratives is through the personal log entries that Snyman performs in acts two and three. This feature is part of the play's "parody on the *Star Trek* and *Star Wars* serials," yet they also identify specific crises dividing Durbanites (Meersman, 2005). In addition to recounting Snyman's dispute with the Dumisani Domestic Training Union, her monologues note inadequate "service delivery, racial tension, [and] economic uncertainty" (D 83). Snyman records the changes she sees in Durban, a space she is returning to after an absence. In this sense, she is both an outsider separated from Durban by time, but also an insider as she grew up in the city. By configuring Snyman as an explorer, *Duped* enacts the kind of subversion that Hopkinson suggests postcolonial SF can instigate by taking "the meme of colonizing the natives and, from the experience of the colonizee, critique it, pervert it, fuck with it" (2004:9). Snyman performs the explorer's role in conventional SF, but as a South African she also exposes how certain spaces remain divided, closed-off, or invisible to a majority of citizens.

Snyman is able to see new perspectives via the surveillance equipment on the airship. Although she is familiar with Durban's topography, she is unfamiliar with the protests erupting in certain areas of the city. This reality is underscored by her confusion over whether she sees "tourist Durban or the other parts" on the display screen during routine monitoring (D 89). Noting the other parts "look just as chaotic as the pictures they're showing on TV of the Joburg CBD," Snyman's comments stress political frustration is spreading (D 89). Moreover, her confusion over which region of the city she is viewing reveals how this frustration remains hidden from many citizens. Snyman's exploration of the city via surveillance equipment reveals the tourist sector "looking beautiful as usual" (D 90). This utopian description contrasts the other regions, which are omitted from everyday news reports as "TV cameras don't go to the outskirts of Durban" (D 89). In doing so, *Duped* uses narratives of exploration to map the tensions in unseen areas of the nation, as opposed to the foreign topography of a distant planet. Such views lead Snyman to wonder "how much longer before the streets are littered with violent protests and calls for regime change[?]," a didactic warning for politicians who fail to address the divisions she witnesses on the monitors (D 83).

Singh's foray into the SF genre avoids creating a simple binary between explorer and the people under assessment by identifying both parties as members of the same nation. Surveillance allows Snyman to document the most pressing crises and note the dangers they pose to the health of the nation overall. However, her distanced perspective also betrays ignorance. From her vantage point the city's problems appear at a macro level, as angry crowds rather than individuals, and national crises rather than local challenges. This contrasts the local views that characters such as Bobby have. Ultimately, Snyman's attempt to reintegrate into Durban can not be accomplished from the bridge of an airship. Her decision to visit Durban's beaches and meet her Uncle Charlie at the play's conclusion suggests integration occurs through individual connections, not technopolitical projects like the airship (D 116).

The Spaceship as a Weapon

Jones posits spaceship icons situated in a "foreseeable future reflect the military origins of real-world space flight" (2003: 106). The militarisation of the spaceship icon is a logical extension of its associations with aircraft, but also boats. In *Duped*, the spaceship's role policing Durban exposes the danger that apartheid-era power structures continue to shape people's behaviours. In Shantal Singh's estimation, *Duped* broaches "the multi-faceted themes of 'Big Brother is watching' as South Africa enters the realms of international politics; the threats of internal security and challenges of maintaining a productive workforce;" among other crises (2013: 18). Surveillance, in particular, raises the spectre of ongoing apartheid violence because panopticism was one of the central ways the former police state attempted to maintain control.

Edwards and Hecht's description of apartheid as a "technopolitical project" that was "erected not only on technologies of surveillance and control but also on technologies of transportation that would allow vast numbers of blacks to commute to work in white areas" identifies a number of characteristics that apartheid projects have in common with the Airship Equity (2010). As a mobile tool of policing, airship technology shuttles politicians like Masimola around, allowing free movement at a time when the country's streets are overrun with protests (D 73). Putting aside this secondary role, its primary function is to carry out surveillance and enforce the law. Notably, while it boasts an array of "awesome firepower," the airship does not deploy this weaponry in the play, even when threatened by Masimola (D 74). Instead, panopticism is its primary means of control. This power structure is reminiscent of Michel Foucault's description of the panopticon, a prison structure organised around surveillance.

Panopticism, as Foucault explains, "induce[s] in the inmate a state of conscious and permanent visibility that assures the automatic functioning of power" (1995: 201). Deconstructing the structure of the prison, Foucault describes visibility as "a trap" that causes inmates to police their own behavior, "caught up in a power situation of which they are themselves the bearers" (1995: 200-1). This is achieved through a tower that houses a guard who can see into a ring of cells circling the guard station. As Foucault summarises, "in the peripheric ring, one is totally seen, without ever seeing; in the central tower, one sees everything without ever being seen" (1995: 202). It is the potential of being watched that causes prisoners to regulate their behaviour. This strategy was adopted by apartheid authorities via systems such as the passbook, which Edwards and Hecht note "began as a modernist attempt at clean, panoptic surveillance [but] ended as the daily routine of an unexceptional police state" (2010). Evoking this history through the spaceship icon, *Duped* proposes the legacy of such violence undermines national unity.

Snyman's view of Durban goes beyond witnessing people's frustration with government failures, it exposes the continuation of racial divisions entrenched during apartheid. This critique arises through her monitoring of Rainbow Beach, a space Snyman sees operating along apartheid racial divisions. Her description of South African Indians "acting as a buffer between whites and blacks" emphasises the continuing violence of apartheid's system of racial segregation (D 90). This event exposes a population that continues to uphold divisions long after racist laws have been dissolved. Although there is no tower, the continued divisions suggest the mundane spaces of Durban have been transformed by the apartheid state apparatus. People assume they are being watched and, subsequently, regulate their behaviour in the sense that Foucault describes. In addition to exposing the challenge of changing mindsets, Snyman's panoptic gaze foregrounds the danger that the new police force will adopt apartheid-era tactics.

For instance, the police force still uses panopticism to exercise control. The crew's primary mission to find a terrorist group operating in Durban revolves around surveillance, a cornerstone of apartheid state control. Although citizens are not aware of the airship, they are correct in assuming they are being watched. In this way the spaceship critiques policing practices in the new state, suggesting they run the risk of maintaining apartheid-era divisions. Furthermore, like Edwards and Hecht's description of the passbook system (2010), *Duped* explores the risk that panoptic control will devolve into police brutality. Examples such as Johannesburg's officials requesting supershuttles to assist with riot control reveals that, when surveillance fails, the state may use the vessel's armaments against their own people (D 88). Johnson ultimately rejects the request on the basis that the current mission is of greater importance, but he also blames politicians for the unrest. Johnson argues it is the country's "politicians [who have] messed up with your lack of service delivery" and must face the ensuing protests (D 88). Such moments reveal how technology risks being co-opted to empower a minority elite, much like apartheid technopolitical projects. It is salient, then, that Snyman describes the airship as "a weapon of mass destruction," a phrase which echoes former President George W. Bush's terminology to justify the second Gulf War (D 102). Her vocabulary reveals two threats the spaceship poses to citizens: it can harm people via weapons and surveillance, but it is also an object America can use to justify intervening in national affairs, a danger confirmed when America seizes the vessel in the conclusion.

The Android

Bobby, an android, is the second SF icon to appear in *Duped*. Although its symbolism is less developed than the airship, Bobby similarly tests the limits of the Rainbow Nation. While the vessel surveys Durban from afar, Bobby is an undercover agent sleuthing out terrorists at street-level. However, the two icons are similar in terms of their clandestine nature policing the state. The term robot, Jones notes, is derived "from the Czech *robota*," or worker (2003: 166). As a tool of police enforcement, Bobby fulfills the role of unrelenting labourer. Johnson begins the description of his creation with the adjective "hard working" (D 81). However, the other adjectives he uses shift Bobby from a symbol of labour to a stereotype of South African Indians: "super smart, takes any orders, he's a brilliant chef, can sell you anything, and he has a photographic memory" (D 81). Bobby's speech further emphasises this connection as the stage directions note he talks with a *"stereotypical South African Indian accent"* (D 81). Through this icon Singh explores crises of alterity and otherness in the Rainbow Nation.

Androids often foreground issues of alterity because, as Jones explains, although they "may resemble humans, they remain defined and devalued by their artificiality" (2003: 167). Relating this back to Bobby, the motivation behind his performance of stereotypes is a result of his programming (D 91). While Bobby's co-creator wanted him "to have the capacity to aspire to be human," Johnson blocked this feature for the mission (D 91). Instead, Johnson programs Bobby to perform racist stereotypes because, as he reasons, "everyone loves a good Indian stereotype" (D 81). Bobby, in this instance, bridges concepts related to SF and postcolonialism through his otherness. As Hoagland and Sarwal explain, "the 'Other' is one of the most well-known markers that science fiction and postcolonial literature share in common" (2010: 10). In *Duped*, Bobby is a non-human Other performing stereotypical characteristics of a racialized Other in an attempt to integrate into the broader society. Bobby's stereotypes are a form of mimicry, a postcolonial concept discussed by Homi K. Bhabha.

For Bhabha, mimicry occurs when a colonised subject imitates the mannerisms of the coloniser. While the colonised seeks to perfect the coloniser's behaviours and language so as to gain inclusion within their position of power, the colonised remains outside as they are *"almost the same but not quite"* (Emphasis in original,1994: 127). The colonised subject's racial difference forms the basis of their exclusion. As Bhabha explains, the colonial subject is *"Almost the same but not white"* (Emphasis in original,1994: 128). Rather than performing the language and mannerisms of the coloniser in order to gain inclusion within a colonial European cultural hierarchy, as Bhabha's theory discusses, Bobby instead seeks to pass as human by internalising and regurgitating Indian South African stereotypes. Bobby's exclusion from society is based on his non-human status, but he is also marginalised while emulating South African Indianness. In this fashion the SF icon foregrounds the othering of South African Indians in the post-apartheid social landscape.

Johnson's decision to program Bobby to perform South African Indianness reflects apartheid violence because, like the passbook system, the scientist arbitrarily assigns Bobby an ethnic identity. Such acts reiterate Bobby's non-human status by denying him the choice of how to self identify. Masimola parallels Johnson's refusal to treat Bobby as a human in the play's conclusion when, after becoming the commanding officer of the Airship Equity project, he boasts: "Once I had an Indian boss ... now I have an Indian slave" (D 114). Such views adhere to SF conventions that present the android as a "futuristic underclass," but they also reveal how specific ethnic identities experience ongoing marginalisation beyond apartheid (Jones, 2003: 167). Masimola's comment reveals he revels in bossing Bobby around because of his South African Indianness, not because he is an android. In this example Bobby has exchanged one position of alterity for another. However, the identity Johnson forces Bobby to adopt leads him to realise the pervasiveness of racism in society, eventually causing him to take a stand against it. When Masimola calls Bobby a "coolie," the android confronts him (D 98). So, while Bobby begins as a stereotype of South African Indianness, his experiences interacting with this community during patrols suggest he has grown sensitive to the racism levelled against its members.

Bobby's experiences critique racism by implying an android, an entity created outside apartheid, can still be othered by its legacy of racial division. In this sense, the centrality of South African Indianness to Bobby's character shows ethnicity remains a primary marker of identity in Durban. Writing about identity and skin colour in Greig Coetzee's 2009 play *Happy Natives*, Anton Kruger notes it features performers playing a range of identities, but "the fact that the black actor plays all the black roles (Mto, Xaba, Prudence, policeman) while the white actor plays the white roles (Kenneth, Chenaye, Jimmy), perhaps shows that skin colour is still very much tied to perceptions of identity" (2010: 46). The android body opens up new ways to think about identity. Although Bobby is versatile at shifting identities, he emulates groups marginalised by colonial violence. And yet this may be a safer option than not possessing an ethnic identity. Returning to Snyman's discovery of racial segregation on Rainbow Beach, Bobby's non-human status means he would not have a space on Durban's beaches if he does not adopt an ethnic identity.

In contrast to Bobby, *Duped* also contains a cyborg. Its body differs from the android because it is a fusion of biological material and mechanical devices. Put succinctly, the cyborg is a human which is "entirely dependent on machine parts inserted into their bodies" (Jones, 2003: 167). While Bobby is an imitation of humanity, a being that mimics human behaviour in an attempt at inclusion, both as human and South African, the cyborg is a sinister reinterpretation of unity and the connection between biology and technology. Originally an American soldier in Iraq, the man's body was damaged in combat and only survived through the fusing of his body with biological material from a deceased Iraqi soldier. In many ways this scenario reflects concerns contained in Manjula Padmanabhan's postcolonial play *Harvest*. Hoagland and Sarwal contend *Harvest* brings "into sharp relief how First World comfort and health is quite literally realised at the expense of the Third World" (2010: 12). It is in a similar way that the Iraqi soldier's body is dismembered in order to revive the American soldier, a clear act of biological imperialism.

The Reconciliatory Chip

Jones's chapter does not discuss computer chip icons. However, in many ways it resembles her description of virtual environments. A central convention of virtual worlds is the process through which humans enter an alternate reality, usually by fusing themselves with technology. For example, Jones points out that some "authors have found a modem-jack inserted into a hole in the back of the skull sufficient" (2003: 166). Like this example, Singh's reconciliatory chip works by placing it on a person's forehead. Shantal Singh's foreword to *Durban Dialogues, Indian Voice* describes the chip as "the standout genius in the play" because it awakens memories of the nation's TRC and juxtaposes "the healing of our nation following the atrocities of apartheid" with "the positioning of our democracy in present day South Africa" (2013: 18). The computer chip is a powerful icon to conclude *Duped* because, while the other SF icons expose the trauma inflicted by apartheid, the chip critiques a post-apartheid project intended to address past violence.

Singh's decision to use a computer chip to explore issues around reconciliation is well considered. This is because computer chips are icons immediately identifiable as repositories for information, particularly in terms of digital memory such as RAM. Conversely, in *Duped* the computer does not store information, rather it shapes a person's memory. This means the device can be used as a weapon. As Johnson explains, once the chip is in place "Any thoughts of exposing" corrupt politicians "are suppressed" (D 110). Configuring the icon in this way, Singh's computer chip raises questions around the agency of victims in national processes of reconciliation. Johnson, via the reconciliation chip, controls the conditions of forgiveness. This aspect is made explicit when he states: "It's time to forgive me," a comment which emphasises the control he has over the witnesses to his crimes (D 111). While this violence plays out in the limited space of the Airship Equity, Singh broadens the critique by having Johnson link the reconciliatory chip directly to South Africa's Truth and Reconciliation Commission, or TRC.

Johnson's claim that South Africa's "scientists were hoping to develop a reconciliatory chip for the TRC hearings, but they didn't quite have the skills to get it right" broadens the critique to a national level (D 110). This statement reiterates his belief that South Africa is technologically inferior to America. But it also cynically implies organisers of this event may have wished to coerce individuals into accepting reconciliation on the basis of advancing national unity. In this sense, the chip critiques some of the contentious aspects of the TRC, such as how some victims were denied legal recourse against perpetrators as a result of the Amnesty Committee. Annelies Verdoolaege records the "granting of amnesty was controversial, as it acquitted perpetrators [who met specific criteria] of any further legal or civil prosecution" (2005: 185). This historical reality bears semblance to Johnson's plan to use reconciliation as a means to avoid justice. By manipulating victims into forgiving his crimes he curtails amnesty proceedings as victims no longer wish to prosecute him.

Singh's use of the chip icon to critique reconciliatory processes also exposes the complex compromises necessary for South African nationalism to succeed. After Johnson's attempt at using the chip on Khumalo and Snyman, the American Central Intelligence Agency (CIA) arrests him. However, the device falls into Khumalo's hands, leading to a debate about whether forcing people to reconcile is an appropriate compromise for nationalism to prevail. The play concludes with Masimola in charge of the airship project. When Snyman attempts to resign because Masimola is collaborating with the CIA, he attacks her. In the scuffle Masimola is badly injured. Khumalo uses the reconciliation chip on Masimola to prevent Snyman from being charged with assault. Although Snyman dislikes this resolution because "[i]t's so deceptive," Khumalo uses the chip so that good citizens can remain in positions of power (D 73). This strategy suggests neither feel that Snyman will see a fair trial if her case were to go to court. And yet, it also leaves Snyman confined to a position of silence. Only she and Khumalo know she is a victim of Masimola's aggression, and neither of them can speak of this as it would lead to her arrest. In this regard Snyman, the victim in the situation, retains the memory of violence while the aggressor is freed through the amnesia created by the reconciliatory chip. This conflict epitomises how this icon raises questions about memory and unity at a time when theatre was exploring crises around the transition from apartheid to a democracy.

Conclusion

Duped uses SF icons to foreground national crises in the early years of the millennium. In doing so, the play remains sceptical about technopolitical projects and the relationship between the state and its citizens. This scepticism reflects the role technology traditionally occupied during colonisation. As Csicsery-Ronay, Jr. notes, there "can be no doubt that without constantly accelerating technological innovation imperialism could not have had the force that it did" (2003). Singh's three icons reflect such tensions as they alternate between tools that usher in stability and weapons that perpetuate imperial violence. The link between technology and imperialism is clearly developed in the conclusion when America, a neo-imperial power, seizes control of the Airship Equity. Such actions constitute neo-imperialism because they combine "the practice, theory, and the attitudes of a dominating metropolitan centre ruling a distant territory," Edward Said's definition of imperialism, with digital technologies to assert control (1993:9). Further conveying this link, the title reflects how characters have been deceived into manufacturing equipment which ultimately serves American interests. The ending reveals America has spied on Snyman in the same way that she has monitored South Africans, a reality which reconfigures technology from solution to problem. While Shantal Singh contends that *Duped* ends by alluding "to the possibility that the chief officers can contemplate some semblance of normality in ordinary pursuits," this vision excludes the technology people have relied on throughout the play (2013:18). In addition to Snyman abandoning the ship for Durban's beaches, she and Khumalo blame Masimola's concussion on Bobby's programming and do not mention the computer chip in order to keep their secret. Although Bobby's fate remains unknown, this conclusion reveals the ongoing distrust people have towards new technology and marks a continuation of his othering. These themes remain topical to South African theatre and, through examples such as **Laine Butler's** *Gaslight,* a 2018 Standard Bank Ovation award winner, reveal South Africans' continuing interest in SF and the ways that this genre intersects with lived reality.

Bibliography

Bhabha, Homi K. 1994. *The Location of Culture*. New York: Routledge.

Blumberg, Marcia. 2009. South African Theatre beyond 2000: Theatricalising the Unspeakable. *Current Writing*, 21(1&2):238-260. https://doi.org/10.1080/101392 9X.2009.9678320

Butler, Laine. 2018. *Gaslight* (performance). Makhanda: National Arts Festival.

Coetzee, Greig. 2003. Happy Natives. In: H. Barnes (Comp). *Johnny Boskak is Feeling Funny and Other Plays*. Scottsville: KwaZulu-Natal UP. 243-310.

Csicsery-Ronay, Jr., Istvan. 2003. Science Fiction and Empire. *Science Fiction Studies*, 30(2):231-245. https://www.jstor.org/stable/4241171

Edwards, Paul, and Gabrielle Hecht. 2010. History and the Technopolitics of Identity: The Case of Apartheid South Africa. *Journal of Southern African Studies*, 36(3):619-639. https://doi.org/10.1080/03057070.2010.507568

Foucault, Michel. 1995 [1977]. *Discipline and Punish*. New York: Vintage.

Govinden, Devarakshanam Betty. 2013. A Critical Overview. In: A. Singh (author). *Durban Dialogues, Indian Voice*. Twickenham, UK: Aurora Metro Books. 13-15.

Hoagland, Erika, and Reema Sarwal. 2010. Introduction. In: E. Hoagland & S. Reema (eds). *Science Fictions, Imperialism and the Third World*. North Carolina: McFarland. 5-19.

Homann, Greg. 2009. *At This Stage: Plays From Post-Apartheid South Africa*. Johannesburg: Witwatersrand UP.

Hopkinson, Nalo. 2004. Introduction. In: N. Hopkinson & U. Mehan (eds). *So Long Been Dreaming*. Vancouver: Arsenal. 7-9.

Jones, Gwyneth. 2003. The Icons of Science Fiction. In: E. James & F. Mendlesohn (eds). *The Cambridge Companion to Science Fiction*. Cambridge: Cambridge UP. 163-173.

Kruger, Anton. 2010. Fashionably Ethnic: Individuality and Heritage in Greig Coetzee's *Happy Natives*. *Current Writing*, 22 (1): 43-58. http://dx.doi.org/10.1080/101392 9X.2010.9678333

Lutge, Debbie. 2017. Director's Note. *Duped Programme*. 11 November.

Meersman, Brent. 2005. Pansa's New Pens. *Mail & Guardian*, 18 November: 9.

Mutwa, Credo. 1981. uNosilimela. In: R. Kavanagh. *South African People's Plays*. London: Heinemann. 1-61.

Padmanabhan, Manjula. 2001. Harvest. In: H. Gilbert. *Postcolonial Plays: An Anthology*. London: Routledge. 217-249.

Plaut, Martin. 2010. South Africa – the ANC's Difficult Allies. *Review of African Political Economy*, 37(124):201-212. https://doi.org/10.1080/03056244.2010.483894

Said, Edward. 1993. *Culture and Imperialism*. New York: Vintage.

Samuelson, Meg. 2007. *Remembering the Nation, Dismembering Women?* Scottsville: Kwazulu-Natal UP.

Sawyer, Andy. 2010. Foreword. In: E. Hoagland & S. Reema (eds). *Science Fictions, Imperialism and the Third World*. North Carolina: McFarland. 1-3.

Sichel, Adrienne. 2005. Wordsmiths who tell it like it is. *The Star*, 17 November,10.

Singh, Ashwin. 2013. *Duped*. In: A. Singh (author). *Durban Dialogues, Indian Voice*. Twickenham, UK: Aurora Metro Books. 71-116.

Singh, Ashwin. 2019. Email. 5 July.

Singh, Shantal. 2013. Summary and Analysis. In: A. Singh (author). *Durban Dialogues, Indian Voice*. Twickenham, UK: Aurora Metro Books. 16-20.

Smith, Eric D. 2012. *Globalization, Utopia, and Postcolonial Science Fiction*. New York: Palgrave Macmillan.

Smith, Johann. 2018. *Gods of My Country* (performance). Makhanda: National Arts Festival.

Thrall, James H. 2009. Postcolonial Science Fiction?: Science, Religion and the Transformation of Genre in Amitav Ghosh's *The Calcutta Chromosome*. *Literature & Theology*, 23(3): 289-302. https://doi.org/10.1093/litthe/frp041

Uys, Pieter-Dirk. 1975. *God's Forgotten*. http://pdu.co.za/forgotten.html

Verdoolaege, Annelies. 2005. Media Representations of the South African Truth and Reconciliation Commission and Their Commitment to Reconciliation. *Journal of African Cultural Studies*, 17(2):181-199. http://www.jstor.org/stable/4141309

SCENE 4

Exploring Trauma in Post-Apartheid South Africa as experienced by Lead Characters in Ashwin Singh's plays *Shooting, Beyond the Big Bangs* and *Into the Grey*

Shantal Singh

Introduction

South Africa held its first democratic election in 1994 after successfully dismantling decades of legislated racial segregation. The world received images of a united country that was celebrating its diversity and for a while the image became a lived reality. However, protracted violence, socio-political naivety, rampant corruption and incompetence became the narrative of democratic South Africa. The optimism of the nation was diminished and what emerged was the undeniable reality – South Africans were a traumatized society.

Ebrahim Harvey, a political writer and commentator, in a scathing analysis of violence in South Africa stated, "That horrendous violence meted out by Dutch and Afrikaner nationalism and British imperialism on black people, since the earliest days of slavery and the genocide against the Khoisan people in the Cape Colony, is necessary to grasp the very deep historical roots of structural, institutional and personal violence in this country" (*Daily News*, September 2019:7). He goes on to state, "… we have been savaged by and internalized not only the violence of our history, but also the violence of what has happened in this country after 1994" (*Daily News*, September 2019:7). The dehumanizing nature of the past has indelibly influenced violent resolutions to conflict but a democratic South Africa has not offered healthy solutions and in many instances socio-political and economic failures have galvanized violence. Crime statistics reported by the South African Police Service have shown progressive increases in violent crime in recent years (Thobane and Prinsloo, 2018). Otwombe, Dietrich, Sikkema, Coetzee, Hopkins, Laher and Gray (2015) studied adolescents from four low socio-economic suburbs in Johannesburg, South Africa and they found that witnessing of community and family violence had reached endemic rates.

How then does society try to make sense of these narratives? If theatre is to play a role then playwrights are charged with the duty to authentically depict characters as they engage with the conflicts of their lives. A playwright tackling the impact of trauma runs the risk of diminishing into sentimentality, creating weak and unvoiced characters and alienating the audience if dramatic undertones are overwhelming and judgmental. This chapter evaluates Ashwin Singh's ability to tackle the complex theme of trauma in post-apartheid South Africa and in so doing examines the authenticity of characters, the relevance of context in an emerging democracy and the writer's ability to balance the emotion of trauma while entertaining the audience. Singh has had two anthologies of plays published, namely *Durban Dialogues, Indian Voice* (2013) and *Durban Dialogues, Then and Now* (2017). Three of the plays contained in these anthologies have central characters who experience significant trauma. These plays are *Shooting, Beyond the Big Bangs* and *Into the Grey*. The incidents of trauma documented in those plays are: emotional and physical abuse by family; police brutality and violent protest action; assault and murder; and institutional neglect and corruption.

In examining Singh's work, it will be necessary to explore psychological constructs of post-traumatic stress disorder and the contribution of drama in the trauma narrative; the relevance of writing about trauma in post-apartheid South Africa will be considered, and the works of other acclaimed South African playwrights, namely John Kani, Athol Fugard and Mike van Graan will be compared to Singh's to evaluate choices that the writers made when dealing with trauma in contemporary South Africa. For this comparative purpose, Kani's *Nothing but the Truth* (2002), Fugard's *The Train Driver* (2010) and van Graan's *Green Man Flashing* (2006) will be referenced.

Trauma is multi-faceted and therefore is used to describe both physical and emotional responses to distress. For the purpose of this article, only post-traumatic stress disorder will be considered when examining the plays. *The Diagnostic and Statistical Manual of Mental Disorders*, Fifth Edition (2013) identifies five core aspects of post-traumatic stress disorder, namely, the individual must have been exposed to an actual or threatened death, serious injury or sexual violence; there must be intrusive symptoms such as distressing memories, dreams or flashbacks of the traumatic incident; there must be persistent avoidance of the stimuli associated with the trauma; there must be alterations in cognitions and mood in response to the traumatic event; and there must be significant alterations in arousal and reactivity associated with the trauma itself. In order to meet criterion, the individual must also have been experiencing the symptoms for more than a month, otherwise it will be considered to be an acute stress reaction. The use of the term 'disorder' has over several years been disputed because any reasonable person experiencing a traumatic event is likely to present those symptoms but the terminology suggests psychopathology.

Bracken (2003:4) believes that "psychiatric diagnosis is often little more than a simplification of a complex reality and by formulating an individual's experiences in terms of pathology it can be profoundly disempowering and stigmatizing". Bracken developed his theories on understanding meaning, culture and mental illness after he worked as a psychiatrist in Uganda in the period 1987 to 1991. Much of the international work done in the continent of Africa would have drawn on Western ideology to understand trauma narratives. In simple terms, there is often an emphasis on the individual when formulating from that perspective whereas the individual living in those countries would more likely be grounded within a social context invested in community. A response to trauma would therefore not be couched as individual deviance but rather be evaluated within a broader socio-political and economic context.

Shooting

Singh's play *Shooting* is about a young man, Jehan, presiding over the personal effects of his murdered cousin, Ishaan. It is a memory play performed by one actor and presents the lives of poor Indians. As Jehan looks through the documents and objects that occupy a space in his cousin's house he recalls the many sporting adventures that he had with his cousin in the backyard and he expresses the guilt he feels for barely knowing him in his adult years. We learn about the multiple traumas that Ishaan had faced, namely physical and emotional abuse by his father and witnessing his father abuse his mother; being abandoned by his mother and then her returning to her children when his father dies; being denied opportunities to represent the school in football; associating with criminal gangs in the area and his unexplained murder as a young adult. Jehan had witnessed Ishaan's trauma when they were children. The story has a non-judgmental undertone and uses tense scenes to capture the troubled mind of Jehan as he tries to emotionally process the death of his cousin.

Singh places Jehan historically in the realities of South Africa where his Uncle Tony informs him and his cousin Ishaan about the atrocities perpetrated during apartheid and then Tony hypocritically engages in violence against his family. Singh also brings Jehan full circle by physically allowing him to inhabit the space of his childhood which later became the home of his cousin as an adult. The artistic devices allow for a multi-layered development of characters, showing the positive attributes, deep insecurities and intense sensitivity of people trying to survive in poorly resourced communities. It draws empathy for the multiple betrayals experienced by youth who were promised a better life in democratic South Africa but were dehumanized by the corruption of institutions and the failings of family and community. Jehan found it difficult to speak at his cousin's funeral and he makes the following reflection: "But I couldn't speak. I didn't know this man. My life had become too busy. But I remember that boy, I remember two little boys. The footballer and the storyteller. I was the witness. I had…I had wanted to be … to do more." (Sh 72). It is Jehan's crippling guilt that he was unable to rescue his cousin from his traumatic life. Singh contextualizes the children's growth with the birth of a democratic South Africa.

Jehan's dissociative responses materialize through his flashbacks of the traumas experienced. He loses a sense of where he is and is brought back into the now by interruptions that come from outside the room which he is physically occupying. It is a clever use of psychological constructs that reveal a traumatized person. Similarly, van Graan's play *Green Man Flashing* (2006) explores multiple traumas experienced by the central character, Gabby Anderson, including the death of her child, the end of her marriage, being raped by her boss and the political party she worked for that sent her ex-husband and a party crony to deal with the situation. The situation escalates and while her ex-husband is taking a telephone call, the party crony threatens her and she ends up shooting him. The use of dream-like sequences jolts one in-and-out of traumatic episodes and contexts, and cleverly highlights that the lust for power can infiltrate democratic societies in much the same way as it does dictatorships. Whereas one of the strengths of Singh's play *Shooting* is the complexities and contradictions of its central characters, some of van Graan's core characters seem to be mouth-pieces for political exchanges and lack emotional depth.

Singh and van Graan place their characters very deliberately within socio-political contexts and therefore the individuals experiencing the trauma are impacting on and are being impacted by their surroundings. It is consistent with Bracken's observations of trauma within an African context. Singh creates the atmosphere of the community by allowing the narrator to physically place himself; by using the sounds of the neighbourhood, for example the loud music in a car driving by; and by using the local colloquialisms. This allows a South African audience to inhabit the space, which breaks the fourth wall and allows for shared realities to be experienced. However, for an international audience, this may present a challenge to appreciate the nuances of the story if they grapple with the authenticity of the language and the placing of the story within the historical developments that occurred in post-apartheid South Africa. It is interesting that Singh's works are being studied and referenced internationally, which may suggest that those are peripheral issues or that an international audience is willing to journey through the lives of another culture.

Balancing complex and contradictory feelings for a traumatised individual is challenging. For the therapist, it is paramount that every opportunity is taken to understand the person and that no assumptions are made about their lived realities. By the same token, the playwright has to be able to infuse life into a character and prevent stereotypes or disingenuous qualities from occupying the profile. Jones (2015:8) believes that "traumatic experiences are constructed through the different ways in which people and groups, cultural narratives and forces within a society make meaning of them and respond to them". It is therefore dangerous to presume that there can ever be a single theory that explains human responses to traumatic events or has a singular intervention strategy. Playwrights operating from different cultural paradigms will organise their construction of stories quite differently to each other, even if they are tackling similar themes.

Beyond the Big Bangs

Singh's play *Beyond the Big Bangs* has three black female characters, each unfolding aspects of their intersecting and separate lives through monologues and dialogues. The women either work or live in a middle-class suburb in Durban. Gita is a grandmother who lives in the area with her family and she enjoys gambling in the local casino whenever possible, Sandra is a domestic worker in the area and Lindiwe teaches at the local school. Lindiwe survived a harrowing incident at her previous school where she was stabbed by a former student. She is now facing a disciplinary hearing at her current school because she assaulted a student who had frequently taunted her and had made a racist statement. Each of the women experience varying degrees of trauma but it is Lindiwe who had a life-threatening experience. Each of the women are confronting their identity as they shape paths in the communities they inhabit.

The ethnocentrism of the community depicted in *Beyond the Big Bangs* highlights the reality that although apartheid has been dismantled, it does not guarantee that societies are willing to engage with each other in any depth. Lindiwe is therefore treated as an intellectual inferior by some of the teachers and students at her new school. This adds further insult for her because she had to leave her previous school due to the frequent threat of violence and the eventual act of violence which leaves her injured and traumatized. Lindiwe claims: "I couldn't go back to that school. That town was beginning to stink…stink with fear and disrespect and immorality." (BBB 210). The loss of our communities to violence and other criminal activities has galvanized greater separatism along race and class divides. Singh brings into context that black-on-black violence also cannot be ignored and that poor governance has resulted in escalating criminal activities in rural communities and a greater drive to be in better resourced areas. Lindiwe's mother warns her about the contradictory and deceptive nature of many of the people in middle-class Durban North and tells her: "You didn't fit into your old school Lindiwe…well, you might not fit into your new school too. Because I don't think the teachers will be different from the other people in Durban North." (BBB 211). Lindiwe is therefore being attacked on three grounds, her gender, her race and on grounds of authority as a teacher.

In Athol Fugard's play, *The Train Driver* (2010) he records copious and insightful notes on how he came to write the story. After reading an article in the newspaper about a tragedy that occurred on a train track he spends a substantial time trying to understand what would have caused the woman to make the decision to kill herself and her children. He eventually feels at a loss to understand it and writes a play about a train driver trying to understand the choice of a nameless person who kills herself and her child on the train track. The train driver seeks out the undertaker to find the remains of the lady and her baby in an unmarked grave but is murdered by a gang operating in the area. He never gets to feel a sense of release from the burden of witnessing her death.

Fugard states: "I had a growing sense that this time I was without any rights to liberty or licence. Apart from the fact that suicide is something I know I will never understand, will always be a mystery to me, there is something about the story of Pumla Lolwana and her three children that would make feeding it to my writer's ego obscene." (*The Train Driver*, 2010: xvi). The result of this conclusion from Fugard is that the woman and her children are referenced but they are not characters who appear in the story. It focuses on the trauma that the train driver experiences having witnessed unnatural deaths. There is honour in acknowledging that the lived experience of an individual is difficult to relate to and therefore capturing the character may lack authenticity. It is also challenging to depict a person who is not the same gender or race as that of the writer. Singh does well in capturing the contradictory nature of the women in *Beyond the Big Bangs*. Sandra's boastfulness about her culinary skills is juxtaposed against her insecurity of becoming a domestic worker. She lost her job as a sales consultant when the company she worked for closed down. Gita's disconnection with her family leads her to become addicted to gambling until she is able to salvage some dignity and considers getting involved in community work again. Lindiwe, having been assaulted in one school, reacts to racist taunting and assaults a student but is able to learn from her incorrect choice. All of the women are presented as layered characters with imperfections and there is a deliberate attempt to demonstrate that they need to engage in self-empowerment rather than requiring men to rescue them. Their imperfections suggest that Singh is able to dispassionately present the women which allows the reader/audience to actively engage with the characters and to determine their own view of these women.

Hough and Hough (2012) argue that drama has a significant impact on brain activation and that it encourages personal development and learning. This suggests that the process of engaging with a play allows one to stimulate higher mental functioning. It is therefore possible that aspects of a play may resonate with a person, challenge personal perspectives and help in a healing process. The women in *Beyond the Big Bangs* each engage in other activities to distract themselves from dealing with stressful or traumatizing situations. For Gita, it is gambling, Sandra enjoys storytelling and baking and Lindiwe loves singing. Similarly, the train driver in Fugard's story, Roelf Visagie explains that he is getting better: "I tried to keep my mind off things by working in the garden, doing Christmas shopping with Lorraine – that is when we bought the Christmas tree – and just anything else you know that would keep my hands busy. I'm one of those guys that if his hands is busy (sic), he's happy." (*The Train Driver*, 2010:15).

Zakes Mda commented in his introduction to John Kani's play, *Nothing but the Truth* (2002) that the play was highly acclaimed by critics and that it resonated with audiences. The play is set against the backdrop of the Truth and Reconciliation hearings that were held in the country to redress past injustices and bring closure and healing to families who had lost loved ones during the political violence perpetrated during apartheid. The central character, Sipho, is struggling with his internal turmoil of receiving the body of his brother so that he can be given a family burial while still experiencing unresolved anger toward his brother. Sipho blames his brother for influencing his son to become an activist and therefore inadvertently causing the death of his son in political violence. The play's strength comes through the lines of Sipho: "I was part of the Struggle. I too suffered as a black person. I went to the marches like everyone else. I might not have been detained. I might not have been on Robben Island. I did not leave this country, but I suffered too". (*Nothing but the Truth*, 2002:51). Hearing those words must have echoed many of the views of the audience. The play, like the designed purpose of the Truth and Reconciliation hearings in South Africa, would have given the audience a sense of a shared history. It was an acknowledgment of the unsung heroes who fought to survive and to raise their families in a time when surviving was the best that one could do.

Into the Grey

Singh's play *Into the Grey* is about the traversing lives of two individuals, Logan Pillay and Sandile Ndlovu and it spans a twenty-nine-year period. When they first meet, it is as students. Logan is studying medicine and Sandile is studying law. They have different views on violent student protests but they soon find an emotional connection through their activism and belief system. As the two men try to negotiate their lives they are faced with multiple traumas that either connect them to each other or draw them further apart. Student protests and surviving clashes with the police, engaging in activism together and tackling community issues such as criminality and rampant drug abuse, the challenges of their careers and the indiscretions that they committed, violent protests at a hospital where Logan works and where Sandile was a patient at the time, losing the influence they once had in the communities they had previously started outreach programmes in, and death and life-threatening illness are the challenges they encounter.

Sandile admits his involvement in corruption and says: "I deserve it. I'm living in the dirty grey now, Logan. I'm sorry. Forgive me." (IG 54). It is his moment of reconnection with Logan, a friend he had lost contact with for an extended period while he focused on furthering his career in politics. Sandile serves a jail sentence for corruption which he commits during his political career and then ends up getting cancer as he tries to reintegrate into society. Logan's sudden and violent death robs him of the opportunity to redeem himself after he is accused of leaving swabs in women's abdomens during surgical procedures. Logan admits to Sandile that he was fatigued and was responsible for medical negligence. He says: "I'm dying in the dirty grey, Sandile." (IG 63). His words ring out like a prophecy because after his utterance he is shot dead by a drug addict. The effect of protracted trauma is quite evident in the fatigued last moments of Logan. He is rejecting the world he once tried to improve with Sandile and the next generation and some indifferent people in the neighbourhood are rejecting him. It is the saddest reality for him that he had a more significant role to play during apartheid than he does in a democratic South Africa.

Into the Grey explores the concept of living in uncertainty. It is quite easy in writing to get caught up in the process of creating absolutes and in this way, characters become conventionally 'all-good' or 'all-bad'. It is particularly difficult to balance writing three-dimensional characters when exploring themes of trauma. In the play Sandile and Logan have to confront the 'greys' of their lives as they negotiate surviving. Similarly, Kani's *Nothing but the Truth* presents people trying to get on with the realities of their lives but their traumatic realities have a way of re-engaging their attention.

Into the Grey is strongly about men. The active role played by women in the liberation Struggle is mentioned but the writer appears to deliberately exclude a female character. Sandile exclaims: "We should all listen more to our wives and mothers and sisters. The men of this country have fucked it all up! We should let more women lead us. They may take us to a better place." (IG 65). It is a wonderful example of gender divisions that pervade society and establish patriarchal systems. There remains a strong need for some men to assert power over women. Violence against women is a worldwide concern and in South Africa some women remain subjugated at home and at work. The play's absence of a female character highlights the need, in reality, to establish gender equality and to challenge archaic notions of assigning roles according to stereotypical concepts. Singh's choice to exclude a female character therefore effectively makes the point that gender cannot be undermined and that men need to recognize their value in society.

The play creates a deliberately uncomfortable examination of politics in the country. Sandile and Logan discuss the African Renaissance that the government at that time purported to be creating. Logan does not feel he is included in the government's vision. He comments on the viewpoint of the president of the country:

> His language is interesting. He speaks so much about race. To me it seems like he wants a clear hierarchy of blackness, in everything. It's far away from the Party's vision of a non-racial society. Look, I accept the necessity of affirmative action. I know the main focus has to be to lift the Black African majority out

of poverty. But there are other agendas at play too. And petty categorization continues as always. (IG 40)

The disillusionment felt by Logan is also echoed by Sipho in Kani's play. Sipho, referring to the politicians he helped elect, states: "How come I am not old to put them in power but then suddenly I am too old to be empowered?" (*Nothing but the Truth*, 2002: 51). He is disgruntled by not being promoted to chief librarian after working there most of his life. The endured, protracted traumas of those characters seem unacknowledged as the newly created democracy rejects people on the basis of which race suffered most and on grounds of age. Zakes Mda comments in his introductory notes on Kani's play: "If South Africa is to survive and prosper reconciliation is absolutely essential. But true reconciliation will only happen when we are able to confront what happened yesterday without bitterness." (*Nothing but the Truth*, 2002: ix). South Africa still faces this challenge as it tries to reconcile the atrocities of the past, the corruption of the present and engages in shaping constructive goals for the future.

With this barrage of negativity cultivating fertile soil for trauma, it is quite a challenge to write creatively and with a view to sharing lived realities of the country. In van Graan's playwright's note he states: "Rather than wait for 'the right time' for issues to be debated or questions to be asked, theatre-makers should provoke thought, stimulate debate, challenge current dogmas and provide the intellectual and emotional space for these." (*New South African Plays*, 2006:172). At some level plays could offer the opportunity to audience members to engage in catharsis as they confront similar issues presented by the characters. The playwright therefore cannot bombard the audience member with emotionally draining dialogues or monologues because this could cause the effect of uncontained re-exposure to trauma symptoms. However, by the same token, the playwright cannot skirt the issues because themes will be underdeveloped, plot lines will be highly flawed and characters could become caricatures.

Fugard engages the train driver, Roelf Visagie in repetitive behaviour to indicate a traumatized mind searching for a cathartic release from witnessing people die on a train track. He tries to cope by engaging in healthy activities instead of ruminating about the incident. Sublimation is a healthy psychological defense where an individual temporarily focuses on an activity which can offer distraction while the individual builds ego strength to cope with the distressing incident. For Roelf it is gardening and Christmas shopping. For Lindiwe in Singh's *Beyond the Big Bangs* it is focusing on teaching and enjoying singing in her spare time. In *Into the Grey*, Sandile and Logan focus on their professions and engage in community work. *Shooting* uses childhood memories of playing sport and family gatherings to celebrate joyful moments.

Conclusion

A writer's ability to hold the attention of an audience by making them cry and then to be able to make them laugh is skilled practice. In *Shooting* we learn early on that Ishaan is dead but Singh is able to balance the susceptibility of harrowing pain with humour. Humour is another healthy psychological defense which offers respite from the traumas of life. In the play, Singh uses eccentric characters like Slasher Sewlal, nicknamed as such because of his perpetual emphasis on cutting grass, and the local gangster Michael Maharaj who requires a translator because it is impossible to understand his speech. Both characters are capable of violence but constantly thrusting that menacing atmosphere at the audience would make viewing the play unnecessarily uncomfortable. By creating the eccentric nuances, the audience is aware of the characters' capacities to exact violence without being overwhelmed by feelings. The characters are also given layered qualities so that there is no polarized presentation of good and evil. The nature of humanity is that we are capable of expressing a range of emotions.

Similarly, *Beyond the Big Bangs* has a flamboyant grandmother who feels ardently disconnected with her family, spending time gambling in the casino. The play then breaks the stereotypical notion of being seen solely as a gambling granny by giving her an opportunity to follow a different path, a path of her choosing, which is to become involved in community work again. *Into the Grey* keeps the two central characters quite serious. It is the peripheral characters who add comedy to relieve references to protracted trauma. In particular the seedy nature of both Anesh Maharaj, a rich businessman who wants to invest in the community and his son, Vinesh, a drug addict, are the ones who offer some comedic moments. However, both men are also shown to be violent. To create a character solely for the purpose of comedic relief runs the risk of the character being viewed as a clown and lacking sensitivity and sincerity. It will also cause a disconnection with the overall tone and thematic focus of the plot.

Erica Still (2014: 188) observes:

> It is worth noting at the outset that prophetic remembrance is not about 'closure', or the end of mourning. Central to the concept stands the assertion that there can never be any such completion; there is no point at which black subjectivity will just 'get over' the racialized oppression that led to its formation. Such a commitment to endless mourning need not be nihilistic.

Still was examining black South African and African American novelists who were tackling the theme of trauma. It is the ultimate loaded gun. The traumatic events of black people's lives have shaped their identity and in so doing have defined them as a community. There can be no complete release from this as it has come to define their narrative. A playwright has to be honest about the material s/he chooses to write about and therefore characters have to be authentic. For Singh,

Fugard, Kani and van Graan tackling a trauma narrative in post-apartheid South Africa, it was necessary for them to contextualize their characters within the parameters of socio-political and economic realities of the country. Singh's *Into the Grey* and Fugard's *The Train Driver* have the darkest tone of the plays but both plays are not without hope.

In psychotherapy every person experiencing psychopathology is trying to process the traumas of their lives. However, they continue to live and contribute to society despite this reality. Within a South African context, it is difficult to profile a black identity without considering the far-reaching effects of apartheid. Even the millennials have inherited a fractured reality. It is difficult not to succumb to such constant negativity and to even seek respite in frivolity. Choosing to write drama and being able to sustain interest in the subject matter is therefore a substantial challenge. One does not write plays for one's own consumption in some attempt to reach personal catharsis. Plays are written for the consumption of an audience, or in the event of publication for the imagination of the reader. It is a communicative device. The playwright begins the process but it is the person observing or reading the words who gives life to the engagement.

A measure of successful playwriting is whether the characters resonate with the people interpreting the art. One need not have experienced what the character has experienced but there needs to be an emotional connection. Jones (2015:4) believes that: "One way to approach trauma is via its story, or its different stories: the ways its meanings have emerged and what this can reveal about how 'trauma' is currently engaged with in its lived contexts". The process does not have to become overly sensitive but it is necessary to feel that one owns one's story. The process of experiencing trauma is that control is removed from the survivor. Much of psychotherapy is about restoring a sense of control. Similarly, plays by creating a platform generate an opportunity for a sharing of narratives and offer a restoration of a sense of self. Singh's characters are grounded in reality, they possess the contradictions of life and exemplify the potential for human growth. He is able to accurately portray people across gender, race and class divides and handles the theme of trauma with respect and insight while still managing to entertain.

Bibliography

American Psychiatric Association: Diagnostic and Statistical Manual of Mental Disorders, Fifth Edition. 2013. Arlington: VA, American Psychiatric Association.

Bracken, P. 2003. *Trauma: Culture, Meaning and Philosophy.* London: Whurr Publishers.

Fugard, A. 2010. *The Train Driver.* London: Faber and Faber

Harvey, E. 2019. We are Violent People. *Daily News,* 2 September:7.

Hough, B.H and Hough, S. 2012. The Play was Always the Thing: Drama's effects on Brain Function. *Psychology,* 3 (6): 454-456.

Jones, P. 2015. Trauma and Dramatherapy: Dreams, Play and the Social Construction of Culture. *South African Theatre Journal,* 28 (1): 4-16, https://doi.org/10.1080/10137548 .2015.1011897

Kani, J. 2002. *Nothing but the Truth.* Johannesburg: Witwatersrand University Press.

Otwombe, K.N, Dietrich, J, Sikkema, K.J, Coetzee, J, Hopkins, K.L, Laher, F and Gray, G.E. 2015. Exposure to and experiences of violence among adolescents in lower socio-economic groups in Johannesburg, South Africa. *BMC Public Health,* 15 (450): 1-11. https://doi.org/10.1186/s12889-015-1780-8

Singh, A. 2013. *Durban Dialogues, Indian Voice.* Twickenham, UK: Aurora Metro Books.

Singh, A. 2017. *Durban Dialogues, Then and Now.* Twickenham, UK: Aurora Metro Books.

Still, E. 2014. *Prophetic Remembrance: Black Subjectivity in African American and South African Trauma Narratives.* Charlottesville: University of Virginia Press.

Thobane, M and Prinsloo, J. 2018. Is crime getting increasingly violent? An assessment of the role of bank associated robbery in South Africa. *SA Crime Quarterly,* 65: 33-41, https:// doi.org/10.17159/2413-3108/2018/v0n65a4367

Van Graan, M. 2006. *Green Man Flashing.* In: C.J Fourie (ed). *New South African Plays.* Twickenham, UK: Aurora Metro Books. 172-221.

SCENE 5

Racial Conflict Presented Through the Plays of Ashwin Singh

Pranav Joshipura

Introduction

Any discussion on South Africa with reference to India begins with the memory of two great world leaders, Mahatma Gandhi and Nelson Mandela, and thereafter it leads to the picture of a multiracial society where people of all races assimilate into various colours of rainbow reality. However, beneath all beautifully and uniformly laid colours of the rainbow are hidden stories of racial conflict, the struggle to gain racial superiority, and a very sad history of apartheid. An attempt here has been made to analyse racial conflict in South Africa through the plays of Indian South African playwright Ashwin Singh.

The official arrival of Indians in South Africa as indentured labourers started in 1860. However, even before that, Indians existed in South Africa as traders, domestic help, workers, etc. resulting in a rapid increase in the number of Indians in South Africa. With that, an altogether new chapter in the history of South Africa began. Most indentures who reached the Natal shore were forced by compelling circumstances in India. After the Battle of Buxar (1764), the destiny of India was set to change with the British gradually taking over the political reins of India. The nation was crippled with natural disasters in the form of eight famines decimating thousands. And perhaps the most important factor for Indian youth to migrate to Natal was, in the words of prominent Indian historian Dr. R. C. Majumdar, "the decay of the flourishing trade and industry" (1967: 799). Indian youth was groping in darkness facing an uncertain future and hence indenture was received as a ray of hope. When indentures left Indian shores, they left behind everything – name, caste, religion, creed, family, society, etc. and earned a number engraved on a brass plate, which remained their identity throughout indenture. In this way, they were consciously removed from the history of India only to carve out a history of their own in South Africa. No one would have thought at that time that this human resource, which had been erased from the history of a nation, would become an important contributor in South Africa through their honesty, integrity and hard work. The indentures' leaving Indian shores is significant in another respect as well. Hindus considered crossing the sea to be a sin – kala pani, an act of polluting or defiling oneself by crossing the dark water. And hence, when one crosses a sea, there is no point of return for him/her as he/she has to forsake his/her caste, creed, religion, family, etc. before embarking. And therefore, the society in which he/she lives throws him/her out of the specific caste and hence the person cannot be accommodated into the same caste again. Returning home means climbing down the ladders of caste. Of course, a few indentures returned only to face problems and so most stayed in South Africa. Such were the compelling circumstances, need and necessity of indentures. And hence, they survived even amidst the most inhuman conditions in South Africa.[1]

Indians in South Africa earned for themselves a respectable position in the fabric of South African societal structure. They even joined hands with the African National Congress in the fight against injustice during the infamous apartheid regime and thereby earned respect in South Africa.[2] Consequently, after the establishment of democracy in South Africa, many Indians were appointed to important and influential positions. Today, in the social, political and economic life of South Africa and even within the ANC, many Indians enjoy positions of high regard. Their present status is thanks to all the hard work they have done since their arrival. However, this is not to suggest that Indians never discriminated against blacks. They did, not all, but many, and in more than one way. Plays written by Indian South African artistically present this reality.

The Roots of Indian South African Theatre

With their arrival in the 1860s, Indians brought along their indigenous art and literature. The roots of modern Indian South African theatre are perhaps laid in the oral stories of legends and characters from *Ramayana*, *Mahabharata* and other epics narrated by indentured labourers to their children and grandchildren in stinking, dingy and unhygienic accommodations in sugar cane fields. Every night, an ideal India, an imaginary homeland, must have been recreated in this tiny little space providing much needed courage to survive amidst the harsh conditions of indenture. The oral story-telling tradition led to temple festivals where dance-dramas, known as Kathakali or Therukoothu, were performed. These temple festivals were cultural and social gatherings which also marked community building processes. People must have gathered there to find their India which they had left behind, their home which had become a forbidden place for them because of *kala pani*, a point of no return, the India which second generation Indian South Africans had never seen. Plays performed at temple festivals were full of dance, songs, dialogues, drama, jokes, interaction with the audience, live music, etc. These plays connected audiences, who readily responded to performance, with contemporary issues and problems. So, what they were watching were perhaps their own problems artistically represented on stage. However, when

---

1   I have chosen to focus on the indentured labourers but of course as from 1870 large numbers of so-called "Passenger Indians" arrived mainly from Gujarat to take up work as traders, see https://www.sahistory.org.za/article/indian-south-africans

2   Naturally not all Indians were in favor of the ANC. Lemon, 2009, discusses the rifts in the Indian community.

school education formally began among Indians, temple festival dramas were gradually transferred to school auditoriums. Initially, education was imparted in vernacular Indian languages as it probably was quite informal. However, as time progressed, the community realised the importance of the language of the rulers and hence English became the language of school education. Such a sensible action shows dynamism within the community reflecting their tendency to change when time demanded. Plays of classical Indian as well as European playwrights were performed in schools. A passion for theatre started building up among children and this is how professional theatre culture was cultivated among Indians. Many Indian playwrights, directors, actors and technicians practiced theatre. In the words of Sathasivan Annamalai, "Throughout the first half of the nineties, theatre by people such as Tommy Lalbhadur, N. C. Naidoo, Swamivel Pillay and Mathimugam Pillay were produced mainly for philanthropic reasons" (2013: 12). However, Indian South African theatre as a distinct genre was established in 1964 when at the end of a theatre workshop conducted at Durban by theatre director from India, Krishna Shah, a trilogy titled *Trio against Trains* was written. This title was selected as the workshop place was adjacent to the railway line and its participants were often disturbed by passing trains. Theatre activists across race participated in this workshop. Legendary playwright Ronnie Govender's *Beyond Calvary* is regarded as of "historical importance" and also as the "most significant development in black theatre" (Chetty, 2001: 247). With that began a tradition of Indian South African drama. And thus, the role of Krishna Shah is considered to be pivotal in setting up Indian South African theatre. Apart from Ronnie Govender, playwrights like Kessie Govender, Kriben Pillay, Muthal Naidu, Ismail Mahomed, Rajesh Gopie and Ashwin Singh among others have contributed significantly during and after apartheid. Apart from works written by these playwrights, many plays were written and performed and were well appreciated. However, a large number of these plays remained limited only to performance as they are no longer discussed and remembered. This is mainly because the apartheid government obviously would not print anything written against their rule as the publication industry was dominated and controlled by whites and censorship was fairly common. And hence, many of these plays could not have found publishers. Moreover, these plays critiqued apartheid rule and its impact on the community through performance. So, there is a possibility that the problems they discussed have stopped interesting contemporary readers. Lastly, these plays were written for a purpose, i.e., artistically opposing the policy of segregation, and when their purpose was addressed, these playwrights must have felt satisfied for the duty they did faithfully without showing any further interest in publication.

Ashwin Singh's Plays

Ashwin Singh is the award-winning, Durban-based Indian South African playwright whose plays help understand the dynamics of post-apartheid South African society. His plays are discussed in South Africa as well as other nations and are performed at various theatres around the world. Five plays in his anthology titled *Durban Dialogues, Indian Voice: Five South African Plays*, published in 2013, reveal intricate interracial relationships among ethnic groups. These plays bring to the fore certain past events of the Indian community from their sugar cane field days to their participation in the freedom Struggle and they also focus on the predicament of Indians in the post-apartheid scenario. His second anthology, *Durban Dialogues, Then and Now*, comprising three plays and published in 2017, shows complexities within the multiracial society after almost two decades of freedom. These plays not only present problems the nation faces at micro level of their multiracial existence but also pose questions to the government regarding their intention of governing the nation. The playwright apparently does not seem to be happy with the turn of events since freedom. For him, and through him scores of intellectuals, the free nation seems to be leading to chaos and henceforth the playwright feels it urgent to reinterpret and redefine the very meaning of freedom. However, Singh hopes for a brighter future. From 2003, with the publication of his first play *To House*, to his latest *Into the Grey*, written in 2017, Ashwin Singh's plays reflect change in the South African society at microcosmic level.

What is 'Race'?

The term 'race' is variously defined, understood and interpreted. Weber believes races stemmed from "common inherited and inheritable traits that actually derive from common descent" (Morning, 2005: 45). Biological features have nothing to do with race. Robin DiAngelo states, "there are no true biological racial groups among humans" (2016: 105). What is generally understood as biological features like "skin color, hair texture, and eye shape" (DiAngelo, 2012: 79) and other character aspects like "sexuality, athleticism, or mathematical ability" (DiAngelo, 2012: 79) are in fact social and cultural differences. 'Race' therefore is a social and cultural construct. Robin DiAngelo argues, "while race has no biological meaning beyond very superficial differences in appearance, these differences have been given profound social meaning" (2016: 102). Such social and cultural constructs greatly affect human lives as meaning and significance of both change as "political, economic, and historical contexts change" (Morning, 2005: 44).

'Race' plays a very significant role in a multiracial society. It is used as a tool to subjugate others. Philosopher Alfred Hoernlé, as early as the 1930s, argued that 'race' is used for the "systemic adoption of 'techniques of domination' or what we today might call institutional racism" (Bernasconi, 2016: 163). 'Race' not only oppresses but also creates inequalities among humans. In this context, 'race' can be interpreted as "the presence of three interdependent factors in the lay understanding of race ... physical characteristics, cultural factors and socially constructed factors" (Dubriwny, Bates & Bevan, 2004: 193). Therefore, it seems "race is not found, but 'made' and used" (Marx, 1996: 180; emphasis in original).

Whiteness

Whites probably invented 'race' to enslave blacks for economic benefits. It seems that they conveniently used 'race' to master, subjugate and dominate non-whites. A racial hierarchy was established wherein whites enjoyed the privilege of being superior to all. Cheryl Harris argues:

> Following the period of slavery and conquest, whiteness became the basis of racialized privilege – a type of status in which white racial identity provided the basis for allocating societal benefits both private and public in character. These arrangements were ratified and legitimated in law as a type of status property. (1993: 1709)

Whiteness became a privileged social position and equivalent to a superior economic, social and cultural status. Cheryl Harris has coined the term "whiteness as property" (DiAngelo, 2012: 85) to explain the advantages of being a white. Ann Morning explains whiteness as property thus, "white carries more than a mere racial classification. It is a social and institutional status and identity imbued with legal, political, economic, and social rights and privileges that are denied to others" (DiAngelo, 2012: 85).

Such property created social class along with class hierarchy. Whiteness means an advantage which is "translate(d) into material gains" (DiAngelo, 2016: 105), a capital to be enjoyed along with unsurpassable social class. Such an advantageous socioeconomic position has created "racialised capitalism" (Mabasa, 2019: 177). Whiteness, thus, has become a canon and a social, political and economic idea which all non-whites try to emulate as it entitles a superior position. Cheryl Harris argues, "...being white automatically ensured higher economic returns in the short term, as well as greater economic, political, and social security in the long run" (1993: 1713). White racism is thus translated into racial capitalism as "racialism would inevitably permeate the social structures emergent from capitalism" (Melamed, 2015: 77). Racial capitalism also means "white supremacist capitalist development, including slavery, colonialism, genocide, incarceration regimes, migrant exploitation, and contemporary racial warfare" (Melamed, 2015: 77).

South Africa was witness to racial capitalism for centuries where whites dominated, ruled, exploited and enjoyed superior positions, despite being in a demographic minority. In fact, apartheid appears to be a product of racial capitalism. However, the racial order was subverted when the nation became a full democracy in 1994 as a new classification replaced the old racial order. However, while in free South Africa, blacks now enjoy political power thanks to their demographic majority, whites still hold superior class and economic positions and Indians and Coloureds continue to play a buffer role. Thus, racial conflict has been converted into class conflict thanks to racial capitalism.

Racial conflict in Ashwin Singh's plays

Ashwin Singh's play *To House* presents the microcosmic reality of racial conflict in South Africa. The play is set in a housing colony, Oaklands, where black, white and Indian characters struggle for racial superiority. The old order of white supremacy has collapsed long ago and the honeymoon period too has passed since its Rainbow existence. Jason, a white retrenched senior salesman in *To House*, still struggles to restore the white supremacy which appears to be slipping away from him. The old racial order allowed his white identity to assert superiority over others as whiteness was "a type of habitus and the norm against which others are judged" (Meer, 2019: 505). Not all the whites were rich, neither did they hold influential positions. In fact, many were like Jason. However, the system set by the apartheid government classified all whites as "equivalent to being middle or upper class" (Gans, 2005: 18). A classic example of the kind of class privilege enjoyed during apartheid is presented by Indian South African playwright Ismail Mahomed in *Cheaper Than Roses* wherein a coloured woman successfully undergoes several medical tests to prove herself white, merely to enjoy the class privilege. However, soon after her reclassification, the nation is declared free and all the privileges of being a white are snatched away. Therefore, she is frustrated and feels uncertain about her future in the changed circumstances.

The present government won't support a white person like Jason who still dreams of a superior class status. Moreover, he doesn't earn enough to address his needs and so commits financial fraud resulting in his loss of a job. Sibusiso, a black lecturer of law in *To House*, explains Jason's attitude, "You're used to a certain lifestyle. Your wife shops at Gateway. You want these nice things. Taking some money from a big firm is okay. It's the way you were brought up. You were always given everything." (H 69-70)

Oaklands, a formerly white area, is now housed by people of all races. This resettlement happened everywhere in free South Africa. In fact, the title *To House* suggests the sharing of space with others. Sunil, the Indian Narrator in *Reoca Light*, beautifully describes the resettlement of races:

> You know, it's funny, my parents, like so many Indians, are moving to a formerly white suburb. But the other day, I saw a white couple moving into Reoca. And

two black families moved here last year. Now this side is that side; our side is their side; their side is everybody's side. (RL 185)

Jason is already upset with the end of white racism in South Africa. Having enjoyed race privileges so far, he cannot accept people of other races sharing the same housing complex, more specifically blacks. Moreover, he is retrenched from his job for financial fraud and is unable to find a decent job. His divorce from his wife is going to cost half his fortune. He is sure to lose the chairpersonship of the housing colony. Thus, he loses on political, economic and social fronts. His glorious white world is collapsing. Jason is more pathetic as his whiteness could neither earn a superior position nor could amass wealth during apartheid, the time when the entire system supported him. Sibusiso analyses him correctly, "You were one of the poor whites. You had an economic system designed to make you rich. But you still failed. Your family must have been pathetic." (H 70)

Jason therefore is more vulnerable to racial politics than influential and wealthy whites. He becomes outrageous and stoops to the lowest possible level to stop any black upsurge and protect his white privilege. Sibusiso accuses him:

What kind of man are you? You blackmailed your own niece. You know what she told me to tell you? That you can go ahead and tell her father about the coloured boyfriend. She's no longer seeing him. She's graduated to a black man now. (H 68)

Democracy snatched away all the advantages. But how can he easily sacrifice his white property which empowered him with so many privileges? He, therefore, has become desperate to restore the old order and yells out, "Enjoy your new seat of power, Mr. Khumalo. I'll have my final say before I hand over chairmanship of the body corporate. Oaklands will be the way it was again. The way it should always be" (H 25). The freedom of South Africa has seen racial subversion. With that white racism ended, but whiteness as capital and social class still persists. Rich and powerful whites like Prof. Hamilton, the formidable professor of law at the university where Sanjay and Sibusiso are working, in *To House* are insulated against racial subversion because of their class position.

The question is, has South Africa become a non-racial society after freedom? And, has racial subversion brought along capital and class subversion as well? Ashwin Singh's plays artistically respond to these questions. Blacks have suffered most during and even before apartheid. They were deprived of everything, even basic human rights. Therefore, after freedom there was a natural reaction from blacks to demand and desire what they had been deprived of for so long. Sibusiso describes his pathetic living condition:

I lived with my mother and father. My granny and my two sisters. And my aunt, with her two sons. In a shithole in Ntuzuma. And every time I wanted to shit I had to follow the queue. So when I came to varsity, I stayed in Varsity

Drive. Renting one small room with Thabo. And Mr. Naidoo charged us one thousand rand a month for that pathetic place. And his two sons would stare at us. So I moved to the varsity residence. The toilets don't work. The thugs come and take over your room. Eat your food. You can't even read. There's so much shit. (H 59)

The condition of blacks during apartheid was miserable. Indian South African playwright Kessie Govender's play *Working Class Hero* narrates how badly blacks were treated by Indians in day-to-day affairs. Not all but quite a few Indians discriminated against blacks. The plight of Frank, the black central character, is altogether unthinkable and painful. He is pitted against a ruthless society, race, system and individuals. He understands everything but is helpless as the entire system was against blacks. In *Reoca Light*, Sunil narrates an incident involving Themba, the black gardener, thus:

Themba seldom spoke. But there was much wisdom when he did. And he worked tirelessly. Everyone was so envious that the snobbish Singhs had such an outstanding gardener. But then one day it all suddenly ended. After a big family function, some of the Singh's jewellery went missing. But who could he blame? He didn't have the balls to accuse his relatives. So he did the thing that many people in our district did – he blamed the maid and the gardener. Conspiracy, he said it was. And fired them both. (RL 169-170)

This is how blacks were humiliated, insulted and dejected in day-to-day life. Indian South African playwright Rajesh Gopie in *Out of Bounds* presents an incident involving a black maid, Togo, who is raped by the narrator's uncle, who is an Indian, and then is driven out of her job after a few months as she becomes pregnant. In such a subordinate position Togo could not fight against the situation.

Such incidents prove that desire for self-respect, comfort, luxury and material wealth among blacks become obvious when freedom is achieved. However, the political majority enjoyed by a handful of blacks has converted into a lust for power. *To House* argues that the post-apartheid government supports blacks, even undeserving ones, to rise. Jason provides an instance:

Sanjay, before you went to Joburg, you said the Durban Chamber of Commerce would never appoint Shabalala as their new chairperson. His excesses are splashed across every tabloid, you said. Well now you know they did appoint him. (H 36)

Racial politics in South Africa is misused to favour a handful of people of one particular race over all others. Such politics seems to have taken an altogether new dimension. Racism no longer appears to be a matter of black against white or that of one race against all other races. Racism seems to have translated to domination and exploitation by one ethnic group or a handful of them over other ethnic groups, irrespective of skin colour. The cycle of exploitation has not even remained limited to one ethnic group, rather it has percolated to individuals, who unethically desire to rise at the cost of others. Such individuals hide themselves behind the mask of race or ethnicity to address their selfish aims. They don't represent anything – race, ethnicity or even humanity. Ram, an Indian married to a coloured woman in *Swing*, is unhappy as such racial politics favours the black tennis player Lerato over his coloured daughter. He complains:

> … I kept hearing that biased commentator praising Lerato. She was the first Black tennis player to do this… and the first Black female athlete to achieve that… and I thought the moron is unaware that by so over-emphasising her race he is doing her a disservice. But then I thought, he's not even acknowledging Samantha Gopal-Johnson in any way… is she not Black also… has she not achieved, despite growing up in a poor neighbourhood? Is she not from a previously disadvantaged community? Is there a hierarchy of Blackness? And I saw her stumble. And I thought, you cheating bastards! You took away her chance to compete. You removed fairness from the equation. (Sw 137)

This is how blacks, ironically only a handful of them, are replacing all other ethnic groups causing racial conflict. Inequalities caused by "historical injustices" (Sall, 2018: 2) are perhaps conveniently forgotten to address personal ambitions. Julio Masimola, the black Youth League leader, in *Duped* proves that personal ambition can even surpass national security. The cycle of racial exploitation thus continues, albeit with a different persecutor. John Brewer considers this as "political racism" (1982: 397), meaning "the rightness of the dominant racial group, which forms the volk, may be elevated to the exclusion of other groups" (ibid). Powerful, influential and educated blacks exploit the political majority to achieve their personal ambitions. Such people even do not hesitate to sacrifice integrity, honesty and commitment while exploiting all available resources.

Sibusiso wants to replace Sanjay, an Indian academic and lawyer in *To House*, with a black academic for the teaching position, which would put Sanjay's job in jeopardy. The latter has worked hard on an article, but his work cannot be published until there is a black collaborator. Sanjay, unhappy with such affirmative action, says, "You are playing games with me, Mr. Khumalo. I can see right through you. You're all the same. Ntuli tried the same thing before he left for Wits" (H 32). Moreover, Sibusiso collaborates with the white professor to win her favour. Sanjay, and like him most Indians, thus is stuck between "black political power and white economic power" (BBB 204). He accuses Sibusiso:

> I think you wanted to get rid of me for a couple of weeks. That's all you need. So you can curry favour with Prof. Hamilton. Suck up to the big white professor. Get rid of the charou. Like they're doing all over campus. (H 32)

Sanjay and Kajol, Indian senior marketing salesperson in *To House*, probably represent all the upright South Africans who are willing to work hard to make a living. They unfortunately become victims of "reverse racism" (Brewer, 1982:

394) played by the likes of Sibusiso. Nasar Meer explains the reason: "once racially segregated societies continue to operate racial zones even while there is no formal policy to support it … (in) post-Apartheid South Africa … racial categories are keenly related to the exercise of power" (2019: 506). Bobby, android and ground liaison officer for Airship Equity in *Duped*, describes the way racial politics operates in South Africa:

> I'm going to distribute these fish in terms of the Fisheries Equity Act. (*He picks up the fish.*) Right. Two packets for the black fishermen; one packet for the coloured fishermen; half a packet for the Indian fishermen. Oh, I'm sorry… there's nothing left for the white fishermen. Hard luck chaps. (D 91)

Racism hasn't diluted in the Rainbow nation. Reverse racism rather has crippled the society. Frustrated Jason cries out, "There are black diamonds on velvet seats everywhere. Our body corporate actually likes our black diamond" (H 36). Instead of promoting the right people, the government is encouraging racial politics by promoting blacks only, so victims of racial politics are sure to resist.

Jason narrates an incidence where "black school kids" (H 52) threw stones at a mango tree in Oaklands despite his offer to give them mangoes for free. Jason tells the reason, "They didn't want the mangoes. They just don't want me to have any" (H 52). Jason's concern is much greater, "… immature kids who grow up into immature adults… and then brutish leaders of our nation" (H 52). Such is the kind of leadership shaping up in South Africa. The country needs strong, committed and selfless leadership which is ready to sacrifice everything for the nation. This kind of nationalist spirit would guide the nation to progress and peace. However, Ashwin Singh's plays provide examples of Julio Masimola, Shabalala, Ntuli, Sibusiso Khumalo, etc. who are empowered and politically supported by government initiatives like Black Economic Empowerment (H 36), affirmative action (SS 142), State procurement policy, restructuring of public enterprises (Mabasa, 2019: 178), etc. Supported by all these, Sibusiso thunders, "in a few minutes I'll be body corporate chairman. Next month I'll be senior lecturer. Soon I'll be on TV talking about the squatter issue. The world will know Sibusiso Khumalo" (H 70).

Sibusiso is taking benefit from racial politics. He contrives it so that Jason isn't re-elected. Jason exposes him: "You're a fucking criminal yourself. You manipulate everyone. You're trying to push Sanjay out of the department. You sleep with your students. You play the race card whenever you want something you don't deserve" (H 69). Sibusiso even sacrifices his beloved, Kajol, to fulfil his ambition. Wrong people are taking charge of the nation, it seems. Doctor and activist Logan Pillay in *Into the Grey* is rightly concerned "like most things in this country, the wrong people are in charge" (IG 60). Absolute racial superiority leads to absolute abuse of power and authority. This is contrary to Steve Biko's ideal of "a true humanity where power politics will have no place" (Mabasa, 2019: 188).

Persons like Sibusiso are opportunists who exploit 'race' to win influential positions and amass wealth. If Jason is undeserving, then Sibusiso too is no different. However, the present government supports Sibusiso on account of his race, just as the apartheid government used to support Jason.

Class conflict

The government, instead of trying sincerely to address basic issues, seems to be involved in a race and class nexus. Powerful and influential blacks want to be elevated to a higher class as it ensures their social, economic and political status as race and class combined can bring "social totality" (Nengwekhulu, 1986: 33), a privileged position, within which class "occupies a central position" (ibid). Attaining class position means enjoying privileges and rights which are denied to others. Thus, racial conflict is now class conflict in contemporary South Africa. Khwezi Mabasa says, "… racism in South Africa is inherently linked to the evolution of a racialized capitalist social order and the power relations it produces" (2019: 174).

Elevation to a higher class becomes the social necessity of the powerful. The combination of political power and wealth creates class superiority. In *Duped*, the ruling political party gifts a private jet and a Porsche car to youth leader Julio Masimola to satiate his race and class ambition. Supported by racial superiority, he now wants to be elevated to a higher social class which only whites enjoyed. Class superiority ensures social, political and economic rights, privileges, security and surety. Such superiority is accepted as white property. Hence, those blacks in power try to obtain class position by emulating white property. Sibusiso blindly copies Jason for elevation to a higher class. Kajol comments, "In the three months we've lived together Sibu, you've bought a new TV, DVD player, countless software and now a recliner... You now have a lounge which is almost identical to Jason's" (H 28). Instead of a non-racial society, South Africa is heading towards a class-based society. The result of all this is "a class-warfare" (Roberts, 1958: 167). Ashwin Singh seems to be worried as the nation appears to be heading towards a "class-based struggle" (Singh, Educational Edition 2013: 24).

Those involved in the class struggle are not concerned about the issues of ordinary people. Rather they are busy in fulfilling their personal ambitions. The following lines by Julio Masimola are proof:

> ...as my father, the great activist, performance poet, and collector of rare coins said to me on his death bed last year, 'Son, some people will say that you don't deserve your wealth, your turbo charged sports car, your Sandton mansion... but I fought against Apartheid so that you could have this. And you have sacrificed so much for the Party... so you deserve more – a holiday cottage in Cape Town, a chance to eat sushi in Tokyo, your own golf course'. (D 76)

Leaders in South Africa are thus engaged in fulfilling their race and class ambitions. In fact, political leaders and capitalists have joined hands to exploit the nation, irrespective of race. They have formed a new class, viz., capitalist class, converting racial conflict into class conflict. In fact, the race-class combination has created a capitalist class, the class of exploiters. Jean Ait Belkhir and Bernice McNair Barnett argue: "There should be no ambiguity concerning who constitutes the capitalist class: all capitalist employers, independently of their racial, ethnic and gender background, are necessarily exploiters given their domination position over labor" (2001: 167). Khwezi Mabasa believes this to be the result of " … neo-colonial capitalism" (Mabasa, 2019: 185).

The question is, where would the race-class nexus lead the nation? Unfortunately, it is heading towards segregation. The Homeland Policy during apartheid was strongly opposed as it segregated people on racial lines. However, after almost two and half decades of freedom, the nation is once again witnessing segregated living in the form of gated communities or fortified developments promoted by the capitalist class. Such settlements perhaps are products of racial capitalism. Matthew Durington remarks: "in a newly democratic society based on an ethos of desegregation, do individuals feel the need to segregate themselves along class and racial lines in fortified developments in a fashion reminiscent of homeland demarcation during apartheid?" (2006: 147) These developments prove that power and wealth are beyond the reach of everyone, even the law of the land.

Hopelessness

Contrary to the power-wealth combination, there are so many blacks who still live in abject poverty. Not only blacks, but also people of all ethnicities are concerned about basic issues like education, employment, housing, health etc. Sandile, a black lawyer and activist in *Into the Grey*, says, " … students are still shouting for the things we demanded twenty-five years ago" (IG 61). The government does not appear inclined to solve these problems. The nation seems to heading towards chaos. Jedison, a mixed-race man working as intelligence undercover in *Duped*, informs about the present situation:

> This country has lost its soul. You have mothers throwing their babies in bins. Hijackers who kill you after you give up your car, your phone, your wallet. You've got black managers who screw poor black consumers every day, without blinking an eyelid. (D 107)

There is frustration, hopelessness, dejection and humiliation. People are protesting everywhere. Students are on the streets for their demands, unemployment is rising constantly. People seem to have lost faith in the government and their hopes for a new, free and non-racial South Africa seem to be rapidly sinking. People are disillusioned and have started suspecting the government's intentions.

Jedison says, "I'm afraid this new South Africa seems just like the old one to me. Oh, there's more colour… but it's the same old indifference and corruption and racism. And most people have come to accept the malaise" (D 106). Corruption and nepotism are two serious issues the rulers must address immediately. Jedison says:

> We have another corruption crisis to follow the case of the Minister of New Technological Development and the Improvement of Maths Marks. Now the head of the Special Portfolio Committee on Land Redistribution is accused of illegally pushing through deals for his relatives. And there are so many people who still don't have decent toilets. Where will it end? (D 85)

For the playwright, the law and order situation in South Africa seems to have collapsed. Things appear to be gradually getting out of hand. The nation seems to be torn apart by violence, protests and demonstrations.

> **Bobby** Some prisoners ran out of the back of a police van and they hijacked the Greyhound bus to Cape Town […] The pro-death penalty forum is fighting with the anti-smoking campaigners over who should give the mayor their petition first …
>
> **Snyman** … Durban is falling apart. (D 97)

Everywhere there are strikes and protests. Because of the government's antipathetic attitude, desperate people seem to have decided to take law and order into their own hands. Snyman, the mixed-race Captain of Airship Equity in *Duped*, reports:

> We are facing an illegal strike. From lower ranked officers and domestic workers … I'm so tired of the Dumisani Domestic Training Union. They want their workers to have tea breaks, cappuccino breaks, smoke breaks, Sangoma breaks… sick leave, compassionate leave, Royal wedding leave… What's next? Special days for cosmetic development. (D 99)

Racial capitalism has led to chaos. It was hoped that freedom would allow everyone's voice to be heard and respected. The Rainbow existence would bring a ray of hope for everyone. Instead, racial conflict has continued in free South Africa, albeit in a different way. Anil Maharaj, an Indian entrepreneur in *Into the Grey*, is disillusioned, much like everyone in South Africa, "Maybe this new millennium is not a rebirth. Maybe we were misled" (IG 37). Power and wealth hungry leaders do not have time to resolve the issues of the common people. For ordinary citizens, nothing has changed since the removal of apartheid. Instead their plight has become all the more pitiable as those who fought against injustice are now involved in the cycle of exploitation. People of all races and ethnicities came together as one single opposition firmly resolved to uproot and throw away the evil of racial discrimination during the apartheid Struggle. Unfortunately, after freedom, 'race' once again is enforced to capture power and amass wealth. Ordinary citizens had dreamt of a new dawn where their basic needs would be satisfied, their voices would be heard as leaders chosen by them are now leading the nation. However, they seem to feel utterly disillusioned and cheated as their plight continues to remain the same. They perhaps have understood that these leaders are self-centred and untrustworthy. Helpless and hopeless people have resorted to looting and violence. One such incident is described in *Shooting*: "Crime, unemployment, poverty... so many of our people are disempowered. But does anyone in government care? Is the struggle legacy in danger of being irreparably tarnished?" (Sh 95)

The nation which fought against exploitation for so many years under the leadership of Nelson Mandela, Desmond Tutu, Steve Biko, etc. and the nation which inspired other nations to fight against injustice seems to be almost on the verge of destruction because of class conflict. Will the nation once again rise to defeat destructive forces? Ashwin Singh's plays provide a ray of hope.

Hope

Ashwin Singh's South Africa is torn between two extremes: abject poverty, strikes, demonstrations and violence; and, exploitation by racial capitalists. Crushed between these two extremes, South Africa's future looks desperate. However, the playwright has not lost hope. He shares the vision of a-racial and culturally tolerant places like "Free-Dome" (IG 21), Chatsworth, Reoca, Airship Equity, etc. To create such an ideal society, people from cross sections of society must come forward. Sandile Ndlovu echoes the authorial voice, "We need an active civil society. We have to fight for our democracy.... clean up our communities... build better intercultural relationships" (IG 61).

Only a sensible leadership intending to solve problems of all the sections of society can keep the promise of a non-racial society. Such a leadership can bring about desired change. The playwright invites people across racial lines to participate in the nation building process. Ndlovu pleads: "Let's change that. Let's at least try. We need Free-Dome now. I've spoken to a lot of people. They're all interested. Youth organizations... women's organizations... business people... and I have some money... from proper investments... nothing illegitimate—." (IG 62)

It seems the nation is gradually rising for another freedom Struggle to overthrow selfish and mean politicians and capitalist exploiters. Activists like Sandile Ndlovu and Logan Pillay, and through them Ashwin Singh and the likes of him, want to expose the power-money nexus and usher in a nationalist spirit among the people. The playwright has suggested innovative ways to achieve racial harmony to end racial conflict. One such is "the interfaith group" (H 65). Sanjay explains the purpose, "It's a mixed group. All ladies, but different religions, different races. You know, my ma and I are Hindus. You too. But no one is trying to convert you there or change your views. And they work with kids, abused women" (H 66).

Anesh Singh, an Indian cultural leader, provides another way of racial synthesis: "Come one, come all … Come share your culture with people from other cultures. And learn about their culture. Let's celebrate our diversity. Let's re-build the Rainbow nation. Tell us your story" (BBB 188). Enthusiastic activists like Lindiwe, a black school teacher, can guide her pupils to the vision of the Rainbow nation. She says:

> I was thinking … dreaming about a place where all these beautiful children, from different towns and different walks of life … could all gather to learn, and share. And my friend Simone and I, and all those other teachers who loved their jobs, would mentor them. We would make magic together. (BBB 219)

In 2018, President Cyril Ramaphosa echoed similar sentiments: "This year gives us an opportunity to reaffirm our vision of a non-racial society – to build a South Africa that belongs to all who live in it, black and white (…) Let us work with even greater purpose to unite our people – African, coloured, Indian and white – to build a new nation in which all have equal rights and opportunities". (Sall, 2018: 3)

Only the right kind of education and the government's attitude can end race and class conflict. Then only the vision espoused by freedom fighters can be achieved. Ashwin Singh's plays enable readers and theatregoers to explore racial and class divisions in South Africa as well as providing solutions to end them.

Conclusion

Ashwin Singh's plays show how 'race' plays a determining role in South Africa even today. The dynamics of 'race' change as the political context changes. Ashwin Singh's plays also reveal how class politics caused by the power and wealth nexus is dangerous to the nation, which appears to be on the brink of destruction. However, the playwright is optimistic that South Africa will once again rise to conquer these destructive forces. He makes an earnest plea to all intellectuals and activists to unite once again for freedom of another kind.

Bibliography

Annamalai, Sathasivan. The History of South African Indian Theatre in Natal from the Mid-1990's to the Present Day, with Special Reference to its Transformation within the Changing Socio-Political Climate. Unpublished Ph. D. Thesis. Durban: University of Durban-Westville.1998. http://scnc.ukzn.ac.za/doc/ARTS/drama/Annamalai_S_History_SA _ Indian_Theatre_pdf. Web. 3 June 2013.

Belkhir, Jean Ait & Bernice McNair Barnett. 2001. Race, Gender and Class Intersectionality. *Race, Gender & Class*, Amazigh Voices: The Berber Question, 8 (3): 157-174. https://www.jstor.org/stable/41674988

Bernasconi, Robert. 2016. The Paradox of Liberal Politics in the South African Context: Alfred Hoernlé's Critique of Liberalism's Pact with White Domination. *Critical Philosophy of Race*, Special Issue: South African and U.S. Critical Philosophies of Race, 4 (2): 163-181. https://www.jstor.org/stable/10.5325/critphilrace.4.2.0163

Brewer, John D. 1982. Racial Politics and Nationalism: The Case of South Africa. *Sociology*, 16 (3) August: 390-405. https://www.jstor.org/stable/42852452

Bose, Neilesh, ed. 2009. *Beyond Bollywood and Broadway: Plays from the South Asian Diaspora.* Bloomington: Indiana University Press.

Chetty, Rajendra. 2001. At the Edge: An Interview with Ronnie Govender. *Alter*nation. *Interdisciplinary Journal for the Study of the Arts and Humanities in Southern Africa.* 8 (1): 243-253. http://alternation.ukzn.ac.za/pages/volume-8/alternation-8-number-1-2001.aspx

DiAngelo, Robin. 2012. What Is Race? *Counterpoints*, What Does it Mean to Be White? Developing White Racial Literacy, Vol. 398: 79-86. https://www.jstor.org/stable/42981486

DiAngelo, Robin. 2016. What is Race? *Counterpoints*, What Does It Mean to Be White? Developing White Racial Literacy: Revised Edition, Vol 497: 97-106. https://www.jstor.org/stable/45157300

Dubriwny, Tasha N., Benjamin R. Bates & Jennifer L. Bevan. 2004. Lay Understandings of Race. *Community Genetics*, 7 (4): 185-195. https://www.jstor.org/stable/10.2307/26679426

Durington, Matthew. 2006. Race, space and place in suburban Durban: An Ethnographic Assessment of Gated Community, Environments and Residents. *GeoJournal*, Gated Communities: An Emerging Global Urban Landscape, 66 (1/2): 147-160. https://www.jstor.org/stable/41148073

Dyer, Richard 1997. *White*. London: Verso.

Gopie, Rajesh. 2008. *Out of Bounds*. Mowbray: Junkets Publishers.

Harris, Cheryl I. 1993. Whiteness as Property. *Harvard Law Review*, 106 (8) June: 1707-1791. https://www.jstor.org/stable/1341787

Indian South Africans, *South African History Online*. https://www.sahistory.org.za/article/indian-south-africans

Jones, Brian. 2015. *The Social Construct of Race*. www.jacobinmag.com/2015/06/racecraft-racism-social-origins-reparations

Lemon, Anthony, 2009 [1990]. The Political Position of Indians in South Africa. In: Colin Clarke, Ceri Peach & Steve Vertovec (eds). *South Asians Overseas, Migration and Ethnicity*, Cambridge: Cambridge University Press:131-148.

Mabasa, Khwezi. 2019. Democratic Marxism and the National Question: Race and Class in Post-Apartheid South Africa. In: V. Satgar. *Racism After Apartheid: Challenges for Marxism and Anti-Racism*. Johannesburg: Wits UP: 173-193. https://www.jstor.org/stable/10.18772/22019033061.13

Mahomed, Ismail. 1998. *Cheaper Than Roses*. In: Kathy A. Perkins (ed). *Black South African Woman: An Anthology of Plays*. London: Routledge.

Majumdar, R. C., H.C. Ray Chaudhuri & Kalikinkar Datta (eds). 1967. *An Advanced History of India*. 3rd edition. London: Macmillan.

Marx, Anthony W. 1996. Race-Making and the Nation-State. *World Politics*, 48 (2) January:180-208. https://www.jstor.org/stable/25053960

Meer, Nasar. 2019. The Wreckage of White Supremacy. *Identities: Global Studies in Culture and Power*. 26 (5): 501–509. https://doi.org/10.1080/1070289X.2019.1654662

Melamed, Jodi. 2015. Racial Capitalism. *Critical Ethnic Studies*, 1 (1) Spring: 76-85. https://www.jstor.org/stable/10.5749/jcritethnstud.1.1.0076

Morning, Ann. 2005. Race. *Contexts*, 4 (4) Fall: 44-46. https://www.jstor.org/stable/24715021

Nengwekhulu, Ranwedzi H. 1986. Race, Class and Ethnicity in South Africa. *African Journal of Political Economy / Revue Africaine d'Economie Politique*, Southern Africa in Crisis, 1(1): 29-39. https://www.jstor.org/stable/23500217

Roberts, H. V. 1958. Relations in South Africa as an International Problem. *International Affairs*. 34(2) April: 164-173. http://www.jstor.org/stable/2606691

Sall, Tikam Liese. 2018. The Rainbow Myth: Dreaming of a Post-racial South African Society. *Institute for Global Dialogue*. https://www.jstor.org/stable/resrep19352

Singh, Ashwin. 2013. *Durban Dialogues, Indian Voice: Five South African Plays*. Educational Edition. Twickenham: Aurora Metro Books.

Singh, Ashwin. 2013. *Durban Dialogues, Indian Voice: Five South African Plays*. Twickenham: Aurora Metro Books.

Singh, Ashwin. 2017. *Durban Dialogues, Then and Now*. Twickenham: Aurora Metro Books.

SCENE 6

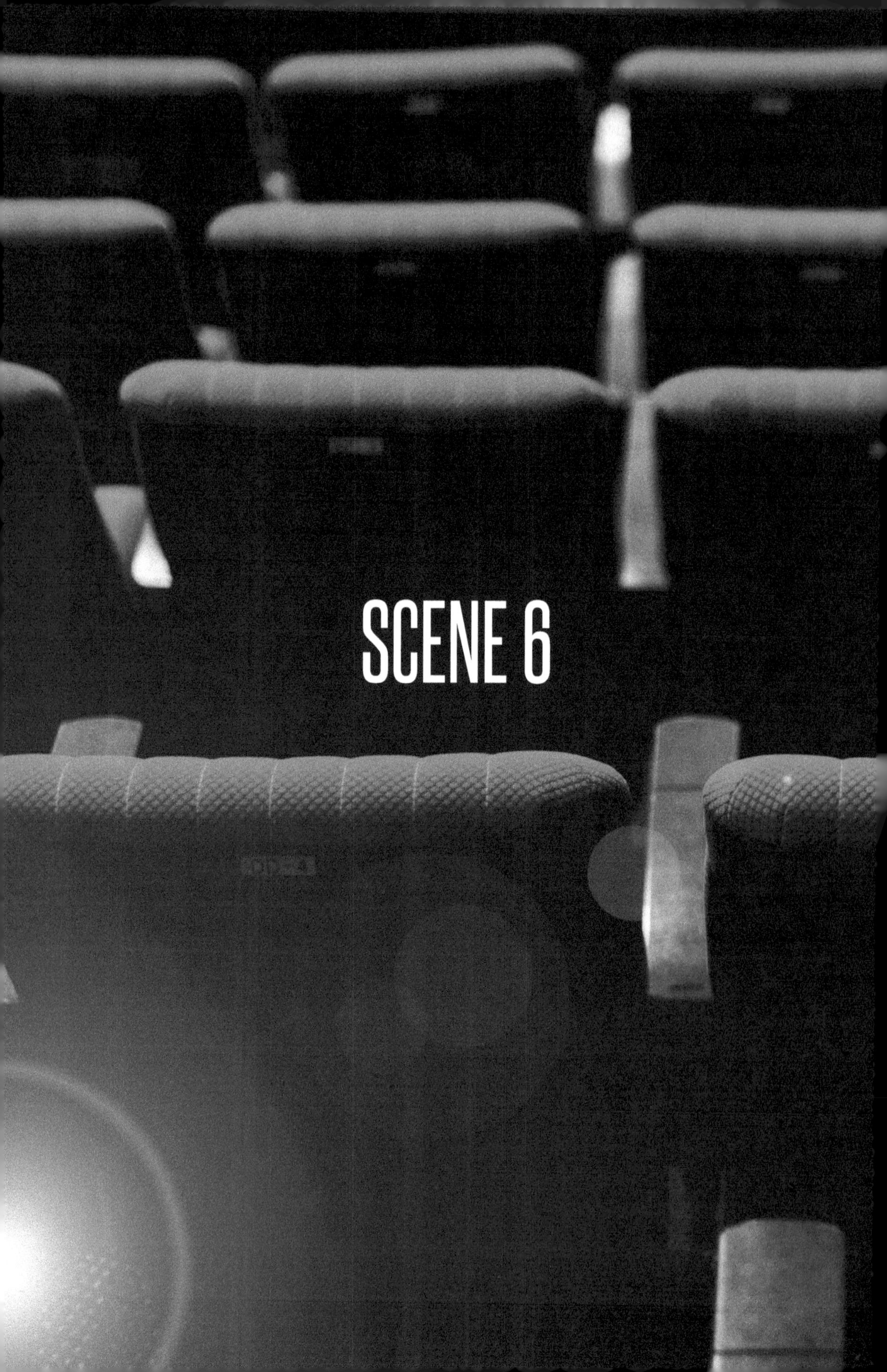

Dilemmas, Disillusion and Resilience in Ashwin Singh's
Into the Grey

Felicity Hand

In the highly volatile transition years from a dictatorial regime to a liberal democracy, theatre critic Ian Steadman argued that

> [w]hat antiapartheid forces need so desperately from theater in these times is not solidarity support against an enemy already in decline, but critical inquiry which is vigilant against complacency, convention, and dogmatism. (1991:89)

He reminds us that "the real potential of dramatic art lies in its ability to teach people *how* to think" (ibid: 78; emphasis in original). Steadman's words ring true as twenty-six years after the first democratic elections were held, a certain climate of national apathy has spread among the black majority. 1994 was what Loren Kruger calls the country's "liminal moment: South Africa's final entry into a postcolonial era" (1995: 60) but rising levels of crime and unemployment amongst the majority black population have not brought the postcolonial freedom and equality that was promised by the ANC. Four years after the publication of Steadman's article playwright Zakes Mda distinguished between protest theatre, which appealed to the conscience of the oppressor and resistance theatre which aimed at "rallying and mobilising the oppressed to fight against oppression" (Mda, 1995, quoted in Kruger, 2020: 122). Post-apartheid theatre's focus on reconciliation still believed in the postcolonial moment but as Kruger points out:

> the current political dispensation no longer lends itself to the clear-cut antagonisms of the anti-apartheid years but demands instead a more complex negotiation of shifting allegiances and representations, historical, fictional, or some mediation between them. (Kruger, 1995: 63)

Almost a generation after the end of apartheid, it seems to me that for drama to continue to connect with people and stir them into questioning the status quo, as advocated by Steadman almost thirty years ago, it needs to go beyond protest, resistance and even reconciliation and move towards resilience.

Among environmental scientists resilience is defined as the capacity of a system to experience shocks – read traumatic pasts, inhumane treatment and unhealed wounds – while retaining essentially the same function, structure and identity (Walker et al 2006: 2). They defend the concept of resilience as the amount of disturbance a system can absorb without shifting into an alternate regime. With this I suggest that post-apartheid South African theatre has left aside resistance and even reconciliation to put forward the need for resilience as a coping mechanism to counteract the disenchantment that abounds in society. One example of this is Ashwin Singh's latest performed play, *Into the Grey*, which debuted in Durban in September 2018. The play had a very short run, only three days, and was clearly produced with a shoe-string budget, but it is beyond the scope of this chapter to enter into the economic doldrums that South African theatre seems to be immersed in. My purpose is to explore to what extent Singh is capable of probing the dilemmas facing South African citizens – particularly those who wield a certain political clout – without losing sight of a way forward. I claim that the play highlights a call for resilience in the face of chronic corruption and blatant inequalities. I will be basing my arguments on the published playscript (2017) but when appropriate with references to the staged version, now available on youtube.[1] *Into the Grey* has a male-only cast with Ashwin Singh playing Logan Pillay, one of the main characters, Menzi Mkhwane as Sandile Ndlovu and the versatile Rory Booth playing the roles of four minor, but no less significant, characters, all admirably directed by Ralph Lawson. The play evolves around three main issues as indicated by the title of this chapter: dilemmas, disillusion and resilience, which I will endeavour to unpack in the following sections.

Dilemmas

Into the Grey spans almost three decades and centres on the youthful idealism of the two main characters, Logan Pillay, of Indian descent, and Sandile Ndlovu, a Zulu, which sours over the years due to various factors, personal ambition combined with political disenchantment being the major ones. The two characters meet during their student days and commit themselves to supporting a multi-ethnic youth centre. As the play progresses we meet the two men in their forties - scene 4 is somewhat sanguinely entitled "African Renaissance" - when cracks in post-apartheid society are beginning to appear and by scene 7 "Free Fall", both are in their early fifties, thoroughly disillusioned with themselves and their dubious contribution to nation building. This first section will explore how this came about through the wrong decisions they made and the consequences that these choices led to. Mike van Graan's play *Green Man Flashing* (2004) poses a dilemma to his main male character, Aaron Matshoba. Should he be true to his principles or be deceived by the lies of those in power. Gabby Anderson, the white personal assistant to a high profile, black government minister with an impeccable anti-apartheid Struggle record, alleges that he has raped her. If the allegation becomes public, it could seriously damage the governing party in the elections. The party sends Aaron to persuade the alleged victim not to go through with the allegations, clearly bribing her into dropping charges. The dilemma lies in the fact that Gabby is Aaron's former wife. While this dilemma takes on enormous personal

---

1   https://www.youtube.com/watch?v=-srEgI9uMM0

and public connotations – gender equality, women's sexual freedom among others – the issue of ethnic loyalty lies behind Aaron's decision. Similar ethnic loyalties feature in Ashwin Singh's *Into the Grey*, which builds on van Graan's play and takes it one stage further. If *Green Man Flashing* draws attention to public – therefore communal – decisions, Ashwin Singh's *Into the Grey* focuses on personal, conscience-wracking choices. Van Graan's Gabby needs to make a decision that will affect thousands of women – as is often the case in rape charges. If she, a former anti-apartheid activist, goes ahead with the rape charge she may ruin her ex-husband's party – a thinly disguised ANC – in the elections. On the other hand, Sandile and Logan, in particular the former, need to reconcile themselves to their previous erroneous stances. In scene 5, significantly entitled "The Caretakers", Sandile, a lawyer turned politician, confesses to not following "due process" (IG 53) in the awarding of beneficial government contracts, interestingly to an Indian family, the Patels.[2] He admits that: "I cheated. I lied" (IG 53). His excuse being that he was promised that "those projects will benefit [his] countrymen" (IG 53). He becomes unstuck when the Patels demand more benefits and Sandile feels he cannot concede any more and, as a consequence, "the party made me the fall guy … maybe I deserve it […] I'm living in the dirty grey now" (IG 54). Logan's fall from respectability is due to his zealous dedication to his work, in detriment to his former activist profile. Now an obstetrician, he blames stress and overwork for a medical error which put an abrupt end to a promising career.

> If only … I've said "if only" so many times […] if only I had focused more on trying to be a good activist and less on trying to be a good doctor […]

> There are two women who have sued the hospital because … because a careless doctor left swabs inside them after they gave birth. […] I blamed the nurse […] but it's my fault. I'm the senior doctor […] I've blamed my staff for my own shortcomings. […] I'm dying in the dirty grey. (IG 62-3)

The passage of time reveals how the pure, honest, altruistic intentions behind the Free-Dome project – "a youth centre and a meeting place for activists" (IG 32) where South Africans of all ethnicities, especially Indians and Zulus, were welcome to participate – are gradually fading away. Scene 2, "Dees Must Fall" – a veiled reference to the 2015 protest movements "Rhodes Must Fall" and #FeesMustFall to decolonise education in South Africa – is the meeting of Logan, an Indian medical student, and Sandile, a Zulu about to graduate from law school. The two young men have to prove their democratic credentials to each other but it is Logan's passionate defence of his South Africanness that speaks volumes about the future of minorities in the post-apartheid era.

---

2   President Jacob Zuma was accused of having a corrupt relationship with members of the Indian Gupta family, and even letting them interfere in ministerial appointments. The Guptas arrived in South Africa in 1993 so cannot be identified as Indian South Africans who have been in the country for several generations. See Madonsela, 2016.

I'm not an Indian. Not as you define it. I eat bunny chows but I don't like brandy and coke... I drink Castle Lager. I don't support the Indian cricket team... I don't support the South African cricket team ... not until there's real transformation. [...] Yes, like many Indians, I'm studying medicine... but I'm not going to emigrate to London when I qualify. I want to serve my African brothers and sisters. Tell that to your comrades next time they mock me again. (IG 26; my emphasis)

It is 1993 and Nelson Mandela is soon to become South Africa's first black President but Sandile has his doubts:

So much of it will still be their [whites'] world. They control so much. [...] Another year of negotiations ... with thieves ... and murderers! [...] They killed our commander ... just a short while now ... they murdered Comrade Hani. And we still forgave them. (IG 31)[3]

Despite their mutual misgivings about each other's loyalties, they become friends after Logan helps Sandile to escape from Sgt Moodley, who was planning to exchange him for the policeman held hostage by the protesting students. Sgt. Moodley, one of the four minor characters in the play, represents the common enemy that unites Sandile and Logan. Sandile taunts him with using the strategies enforced by the apartheid police, "why don't you call for the boys in khaki? Tell them to bring their Casspirs and use us for target practise again" (IG 23). Significantly it is Sandile, not Logan, who reminds the audience of the apartheid-era state repression. The implication is that Logan is more of an armchair activist whereas Sandile was one of those people who became physically involved and often ended up hurt. The partnership that the two forge is perhaps doomed to fail from the start.

Scene 4, "African Renaissance" takes place on New Year's Day 2000. Free-Dome is flourishing, in Logan's words, "We made something special, my friend. Something simple ... but meaningful" (IG 38). However, the idealistic foundations the new nation was built on that brought the two friends together during the student protests are beginning to crumble. Sandile accuses Logan of losing interest in the Party's advisory committee. Logan's excuses that his work is demanding and his "primary job" must take priority don't convince Sandile. In fact, Logan admits he is opting out as he explains:

I mean ...look, your colleagues on the committee don't see me the way you do. They see a middle class Indian medical professional. They make the usual assumptions. [...] when you're gone, your Party pals shut me down. Or they look at my suggestions with such mistrust that I wonder if they think I'm a spy for the opposition. (IG 39)

---

3   Chris Hani was the leader of the South African Communist Party and chief of staff of
    uMkhonto we Sizwe. He was assassinated by a sympathiser of the Conservative opposition
    on 10th April 1993.

Logan's arguments foreshadow the ethnic favouritism that would discredit the post-apartheid governments.[4] Singh's creation of the two main characters as members of different but clearly recognisable ethnic groups serves to underline the focus of the play, which evolves from youthful idealism to gradual cynicism through to – as I argue in the final section – a resilient determination to make things work despite all. The play would not make sense if the characters' ethnicities were inverted, after all, blacks are the majority ethnic group in South Africa and Zulus are the predominant group in KwaZulu-Natal.[5] There may also be on the playwright's part a subtle reminder of what Thomas Blom Hansen refers to as "the larger and difficult issues of the future of Indians in the country, the relationship with Africans, and so on, [which] remain difficult to discuss. Most Indians shy away from these subjects, even in informal conversations" (2005:312).

Sandile is the political animal, the one who ends up burning his fingers and spending four years in prison for his misdemeanours. On the other hand, Logan, who immerses himself in his work, is disgraced but merely suspended.

Disillusion

Scene 4 highlights the disillusion that has already replaced the harmony and goodwill following the demise of apartheid. Betrayal reveals itself as the other side of the commitment coin, so easily flipped over when convenient and economically enticing. The widening gap between the unemployed youth and the new black elite is leading to growing tensions as the Struggle rhetoric and post-apartheid reality seems to have been inexorably torn asunder. It is New Year's Day 2000, only six years after the first democratic elections but Logan, as a member of a minority community, sees through the party discourse. He still believes in the ideals of Free-Dome:

> I want no part of [petty party politics]. I want to continue with what we're doing at Free-Dome. Building relationships with different communities, fighting racism, giving youth a voice… You [Sandile] and I still have a lot of work to do together. (IG 40)

Apart from the name itself, Free-Dome is an icon of loyalty, solidarity and friendship and above all a site for true multi-ethnic interactions. Logan is still at this point – he is now 32 years old – a firm believer in a non-racial South Africa but he begins to query the honesty and integrity of the (unnamed) President.[6]

---

4 See Walters et al for an economic survey of ethnic favouritism in post-apartheid South Africa.
5 According to the 2011 census 11 million Zulus live in South Africa, which corresponds to 23% of the total population. See https://minorityrights.org/minorities/zulus/
6 Given the carefully provided chronology, it is difficult not to presume that the unnamed President is Thabo Mbeki who was accused of promoting economic policies that only benefited a small black elite.

He speaks so much about race. To me it seems like he wants a clear hierarchy of blackness, in everything. It's far away from the Party's vision of a non-racial society. Look, I accept the necessity of affirmative action. I know the main focus has to be to lift the Black African majority out of poverty. But there are other agendas at play too. And petty categorization continues as always. (IG 40)

Sandile's earnest denial of any ethnic favouritism, "He has to break White monopoly capital. And empower Black youth" fails to satisfy Logan's fears as he laments that "[t]he honeymoon is over. We're going into the grey" (IG 40). It is curious to ponder over Singh's use of "grey" to indicate a murky, corrupt area, whereas for many authors the greying of Johannesburg refers to illegal racial residential integration, thus lacking such a negative connotation (Pickard-Cambridge, 1989; Kruger, 2001: 233). Whereas greyness in Singh's vocabulary points to those shady areas that fall outside a democratic government framework, the essential indeterminacy of the colour – neither black nor white – alludes to the much desired social readjustment heralded by the euphoria of the 1994 elections.

Scene 5, "The Caretakers" brings us to the year 2011. Sandile is in a public hospital and is being harassed by a male nurse, Robbie Philander in the midst of a nurses' strike. Singh makes it very clear in the stage directions that the nurse is mixed-race, adding another ingredient to the already hybrid society. Coloureds, as mixed-race people were categorised under apartheid, used to occupy and still occupy an ambiguous position in South Africa. Many of them are Afrikaans speakers, which strikes a discordant note as Afrikaans tends to be associated with the former oppressive regime. Whereas before they were neither black enough to be part of the oppressed majority nor white enough to reap the benefits of the privileged minority, now Nurse Philander seems determined to punish Sandile for belonging to the now affluent and powerful black majority.

I have to hide here. If Robbie sees me... he thinks I'm an easy target cos I'm the MP accused of corruption and he's the unappreciated nurse who's overworked and underpaid. (IG 45)

Nurse Philander's violent attitude towards Sandile, who he regards as one of the black elite, is not the playwright's attack on the former coloured community, who see themselves as displaced and forgotten in the new regime, but a vindication of the working classes – in this particular case nurses in the public health system. Singh is careful to name the woman who is now "on the rampage. Breaking equipment, smashing computers, shouting obscenities" (IG 48) as Head Nurse Vilakazi, an obviously Zulu name, thus subscribing the protest to class rather than ethnic issues. However, his stage directions that demand that Nurse Philander should be "mixed-race" (IG 41) may be due to a recognition of the sociopolitical in-betweenness of the coloureds in post-apartheid South Africa. The play somehow implies that, despite the desire to move beyond these racial classifications, there is no real strategy that allows them to simply be erased.

The stage production of *Into the Grey* (Durban 2018) demanded the physical ageing of the two main characters and a rapid change of characters for Rory Booth, in charge of the roles of the policeman, the nurse, (father) Anil Maharaj and (son) Vinesh Maharaj. Like much South African theatre, typical of the seventies and eighties, the performance included verbal comedy – for example the audience laughs at Logan's definition of Indianness, cited in the section on dilemmas (IG 26) and even in the final scene after Logan has been killed by Vinesh Maharaj, there were hearty chuckles at his father's references to his karma and dharma (IG 65). The businessman Anil Maharaj in his "millennium message" (scene 3) and his son Vinesh in scene 6 "Free-Dome Now" provide the comic relief both in the content of their monologues and in their exaggerated Indian accents. The spontaneous laughter that responded to these characters' speeches may have been due to Thomas Blom Hansen's claim that *charou* culture is "the object of both intense enjoyment and simultaneous disavowal" (2005: 303). The Durban audience would have been predominantly Indian or sympathetic to this ethnic group's position in contemporary South Africa.[7] Logan's failure to carry on the Struggle – Anil Maharaj seems a weak and ineffectual substitute – points to Singh's design to shy away from rigid ethnic categories. He prefers Sandile to lead the new project, if his health allows him. In this respect, the distinguished Indian South African playwright Muthal Naidoo claims:

> I realize that many South Africans like myself, who not only reject the notion of fixed culture but also the notion of fixed identity, are caught in the contradiction between our non-racial aspirations and the pressure to acknowledge if not assert an ethnic affiliation because race is still a major factor in our thinking in South Africa. (1997: 39)

Therefore, and despite Naidoo's words, *Into the Grey* should not be seen as an example of the traditional Indian theatre that Hansen wrote about in 2000 where "the audiences for many [Indian] plays are still completely racially segmented" as the play does in fact "transcend ethnically defined audiences" (2000:266) and appeals to a culturally hybrid audience as well as tapping into an established African way of doing theatre. Despite Yvette Hutchison's claim that audiences in South Africa are "[p]assive onlookers rather than active participants and the theatre is not seen as a forum for debate" because of the lack of "the communal interaction typical of traditional African performances" (1996: 483), her argument that audiences in South Africa are "detached, because they are not homogeneous, culturally, communally and even linguistically" is not sustained as the laughter mentioned above acts as both critique and self-defence. Moreover, following actor and director Janet Suzman's words that "the theatre remains the one orderly forum where you freely choose to plant your butt to take part in an attempt at

---

7   Indians make up 2.6 % of the population of South Africa, the majority of whom live in KwaZulu-Natal and in particular Durban. See Mid-Year Population Estimates www.statssa.gov.za 2019.

understanding the world" (2014:162), Singh's plays pose many questions that the audience takes home with them to ponder over following the Brechtian distancing or alienation effect (*Verfremdungseffekt*). Likewise, the impersonation of multiple characters – in this case one actor playing four clearly differentiated roles – coupled with the minimal props used in the performance harks back to the testimonial theatre described by Kruger (2020: 121) thus embedding the play within a longer and inclusive South African tradition.

Physical violence abounds in much of the play, between Sgt. Moodley and the two students in scene 2; Anil Maharaj's off-stage beating of his wife at the New Year's Eve party the night before in scene 4; Nurse Philander's frustrated attack on Sandile and Logan's response in scene 5; and especially Vinesh's murder of Logan in scene 7, all of which reflect the rise in senseless crime – often drug-related – and gender violence in South African society today.[8] The excess of stage violence suggests a link with earlier performances which demanded a reaction from the audience along the lines outlined by Hutchison (1996; Kruger, 2020: 148).

Violence may have had a political end during the apartheid days, as intimated in Sandile's speech in scene 2:

> Our thugs! Appointed by us to make sure that all students join our protest action … to show everyone that we are united. You see, I don't give a shit if they were scared. They benefit from all the gains we work tirelessly for. We work for the privileged who are always so intimidated when we simply ask them to stand with us. (IG 24-5)

However, Vinesh's murder of Logan can only be attributed to the boy's drug addiction and fear of being imprisoned for arson. Clearly Sandile and Logan are not the only ones who are in the dirty grey, although they have a certain amount of responsibility for being political or social leaders.

The central scene, ("The Caretakers") explores the characters' internal coherence and uses Nurse Philander, plus the off-stage Head Nurse Vilakazi and the security guard Mandla – "such a cheerful chap usually" (IG 48) – as members of the population left on the margins of the Rainbow Nation. Nurse Philander poignantly asks Sandile: "and what do you know of humanity? What humanity do you show when you so easily misuse public funds …and keep us in a daily battle for survival?" (IG 52). Whites are conspicuously absent from the text, either on- or off-stage so the blame for the failure of a cohesive nation is left at the door of the black majority. The allure of whiteness appears to be minimised in the play but what it represents cannot be completely ignored as Pranav Joshipura discusses in his chapter (See also Rose, 2015: 154-155).

---

8   According to https://africacheck.org/factsheets/factsheet-south-africas-crime-statistics-for-2019-20/ an average of 116 rapes were committed and 58 people were murdered every day.

By 2011, thoroughly disillusioned, Logan accuses Sandile of doing nothing for the community:

> You made nothing of substance. You manipulated and deceived and made misery. ... for everyone. And you kept partying. Then you had your ultimate big, fat World Cup party. And now you have this [barbarism] ... all over the country. (IG 50)

Sandile seems to come across as the one who most failed in his original idealistic projects. Logan complains of his inaccessibility:

> I listened to you speak at rallies…and then begged your PA for just a minute of your time ... but no ...you were too busy. And then I watched you on television ... and I heard the language of the seasoned politician ... and I said ... he's become the fat cat that he said he would never become. (IG 46)

Sandile's fall into corruption is contrasted with Logan's passive acceptance of the failure of his and Sandile's – and Summaya's – project.

> Look, I'm not a cynic. [...] But like with most things in this country, the wrong people are in charge ... and they ... what I'm saying is .. .my Free-Dome project here is finished. (IG 60)

The scene ends with a full confession from both parties, not so much of their weaknesses and failings but of how they could still "fight for our democracy ... clean up our communities" (IG 62). This – I argue – is how the play functions as a call for resilience.

Resilience

Sandile in scene 7, the year 2017, is already seriously ill but he is the one who insists on doing something unlike Logan, who is cynical of Anil Maharaj's project of rebuilding the burnt down Free-Dome. Sandile rebukes Logan's excuse that "the wrong people are in charge", he insists that "there are enough people who care, fighting back to make a difference" (IG 59-60). In this scene it is the conservative Indian who abandons the Struggle and the earnest Zulu - despite his illness - the one to carry on the Struggle. While it is counterproductive to analyse the characters in ethnic terms, their fears and reactions are seen to obey their cultural background – Logan reminds Sandile back in 1993 that he "know[s] Indian conservatism better than you" (IG 26). Singh seems to suggest that it is the responsibility of the black majority to lay the foundation of a truly egalitarian, multi-racial nation.

Resilience, which we can understand as being a higher degree of resistance, has been defined in several disciplines, those of environmental scientists and psychologists being the most frequently cited. A simple definition is that a person who can bounce back after enduring some adversity exhibits resilience but Iacoviello & Charney (2014:2) state that resilience, as a psychosocial construct, "is generally described as adaptive characteristics of an individual to cope with and recover from (and sometimes even thrive after) adversity". Social scientists in turn argue that the term is far more complex than is often thought. They claim that "[w]hen defining resilience, little attention is paid to issues of agency, conflict, inequality, and power that shape and reshape social processes and co-determine their outcomes" (Shrestha, 2019: 494). I wish to hone in on the term "inequality" as despite the absence of women characters and their response to the post-apartheid idealism, the play hints at a renewed future and a way forward for Free-Dome, which as mentioned above, represents the interracial harmony the Rainbow Nation heralded. The final scene is entitled "Restoration" but I would argue that what the play claims is how communities can move on and forge a better future, in other words, not a return to the past but an example of resilience. Kruger (1995: 62) argues that "[r]esistance theatre may be distinguished from protest theatre by its stress on the representation or at least assertion of defiance over and above the portrayal of suffering". Protest and resistance theatre lose their impetus in what is supposedly a democracy, despite the social inequalities that render South Africa one of the countries in the world with the widest gap between the rich and the poor (Scott, 2019). However, a theatre of resilience, such as Singh's *Into the Grey*, despite its sombre staging – excessively dark and monochromatic[9] – hints at the way forward if the corruption of the past and the misplaced ethnic loyalties can be sanitized. This, surely, is bouncing back to an improved, more articulated social and political network.

Into the Grey traces the human failings of its two main characters, Sandile and Logan, but disregards the life choices of Summaya Hoosen, leaving women leaders and activists in the margins of the plot although Summaya is praised as being possibly "the best of us" (IG 49). Logan's suggestion that she "just got on with the work [in Free-Dome]" and only abandoned the project because "she was beginning to feel that some of the new male recruits didn't value her contributions" (IG 49) skirts around the gender discrimination suffered by many female activists. Their thoughts, hopes and initiatives tend to be submerged underneath the highly masculinized world of the male freedom fighter (Gqola, 2011).[10] In the opening monologue where Logan berates the Indian community for standing by and allowing a black boy to suffer the consequences of a fire that was inadvertently started by the carelessness of a group of Indians, he claims he told Summaya that she should address the youths in the crowd. She, apparently, said "she wants to listen... that I'm the talker" (IG 20). Thus, right from the very first scene,

---

9   See https://www.youtube.com/watch?v=-srEgI9uMM0
10 This is not an exclusively South African phenomenon as Irish members of *Cumann na mBan* (The Women's Council) often found themselves restricted to mundane tasks like making the tea, see Ryan, 1995. Likewise, Indian women's efforts in the freedom struggle were not compensated after independence, see Liddle & Joshi 1986.

Summaya, and by extension, female activists are relegated to a secondary role, that of listeners, faithful supporters but rarely leaders. Former Constitutional Court judge and anti-apartheid activist Albie Sachs writes that

> [i]t is a sad fact that one of the few profoundly non-racial institutions in South Africa is patriarchy. Amongst the multiple chauvinisms which abound in our country, the male version rears itself with special and equal vigour in all communities. (1990: 53)

The closing scene between Sandile and Maharaj after Logan's murder, is a little overdone in its political correctness, as though the playwright felt he had to make amends for not casting any female characters. In his speech Sandile echoes the character Jake in Aziz Hassim's novel *The Lotus People*, a highly respected member of *uMkhonto we Sizwe*, who acknowledges that women were playing a vital role in the Struggle: "They're the real fighters. Put them in the front line…" (Hassim, 2002: 415). Sandile regrets having allowed a patriarchal sense of male superiority get the better of him:

> I should have listened more to my mother … when she warned me about some of my Party colleagues, years ago. We should all listen more to our wives and mothers and sisters. The men of this country have fucked it all up! We should let the women lead us. They may take us to a better place. (IG 65)

Although Summaya lurks in the background as a shadowy reminder of women's contribution to the Struggle, she is simply talked about but we never actually hear her voice. Logan also makes it very clear in his opening monologue that the idea of calling the new youth centre Free-Dome is his idea, "not Summaya's" (IG 21). Despite Logan's insistence on his initiative as far as the name of the new centre is concerned, in his opening monologue he admits that Summaya has clear ideas about how to proceed:

> Let's do what Summaya suggests. Let's not wait for the dilly-dallying elders in our community. Let youth take the initiative. We'll invite Bheki's family to come here for what Summaya calls a restorative justice process. (IG 21)

The absent Summaya calls for restoration but *Into the Grey* makes a plea for resilience, which as defined by Adger (2000: 347) constitutes "the ability of groups or communities to cope with external stresses and disturbances as a result of social, political, and environmental change", a clear description of the upheavals following the demise of apartheid and the establishment of a democratic government, a new constitution and an end to racial segregation and discrimination.

Ally's Take-away was known to Sandile before he became friends with Logan and significantly it is the place where he and Anil Maharaj enter at the end of the play. "Some things do last" (IG 66) is not just Sandile's tribute to Ally's catering skills but a declaration of intentions. He is a sick man, he tells Maharaj that the chemotherapy is not working, but he remains defiant. In an intent to turn Logan's untimely death and his son's imprisonment into what Janet Suzman called "a joyous trauma" (2014: 163), Maharaj wants to rebuild Free-Dome "in the original way that you and Logan and Summaya were doing" (IG 65). By dealing with the tragedy in a positive way, represented by the reopening of the multi-ethnic youth club, he can actually give himself – and by extension Sandile – a second chance to prove themselves. Logan's death can serve as a catalyst to rekindle the buried illusions that Nelson Mandela's inauguration promised to so many South Africans of all colours and ethnicities.

The rise in violent crime, unemployment and, despite being posterior to the publication and performance of *Into the Grey*, the disastrous outcomes of the COVID 19 pandemic, outlined in Deborah Lutge's chapter, call for an exercise in resilience as the reappraisal of new tragic situations implies a desire to find meaning and positive outcomes. This suggests that even the most traumatic experience, if dealt with in a positive way, can actually provide an opportunity for personal development (Robinson & Carson, 2016: 117). Logan's murder by a young man addicted to drugs and a hedonistic lifestyle, coupled with Sandile's grave illness – he has prostate cancer – should not be taken as a sign that all is lost and nothing can be solved. The play ends on a low-key almost humorous note, that "Some things do last" (IG 66), suggesting that friendship, loyalty and perseverance can take the country forward. I claim that plays like Ashwin Singh's *Into the Grey* can pave the way for more positive, resilient solutions to contemporary inequalities and can serve as antidotes for more positive thinking and a clear determination to abandon the grey.

Bibliography

Adger, W. N. 2000. Social and Ecological Resilience: Are They Related? *Progress in Human Geography* 24 (3): 347-364.

Gqola, Pumla Dineo. 2011. Unconquered and Insubordinate: Embracing Black Feminist Intellectual Activist Legacies. In: X. Mangcu (ed). *Becoming Worthy Ancestors: Archive, Public Deliberation and Identity in South Africa*. Johannesburg: Wits University Press, 2011. 67-88. https://doi.org/10.18772/22011085324.8

Hansen, Thomas Blom. 2000. Plays, Politics and Cultural Identity Among Indians in Durban. *Journal of Southern African Studies*, 26 (2) June: 255-269.

Hansen Thomas Blom. 2005. Melancholia of Freedom: Humour and Nostalgia among Indians in South Africa. *Modern Drama*, 48 (2) Summer: 297-315 https://doi.org/10.1353/mdr.2005.0027

Hassim, Aziz. 2002. *The Lotus People*. Johannesburg: STE.

Hutchison, Yvette. 1996. An Introductory Placing of South African Theatre in the African Context. *Journal of Literary Studies*. 12 (4) December: 470-486.

Iacoviello, Brian M. & Dennis S. Charney. 2014. Psychosocial facets of resilience: implications for preventing post trauma psychopathology, treating trauma survivors, and enhancing community resilience. *European Journal of Psychotraumatology*, 5 (1): 23970. https://doi.org/10.3402/ejpt.v5.23970

Kruger, Loren. 1995. The Uses of Nostalgia: Drama, History, and Liminal Moments in South Africa. *Modern Drama*, 38 (1) Spring: 60-70.

Kruger, Loren. 2001. Theatre, Crime, and the Edgy City in Post-Apartheid Johannesburg. *Theatre Journal* 53 (2) Theatre and the City, May: 223-252.

Kruger, Loren. 2020. *A Century of South African Theatre*. London: Methuen.

Liddle, Joanna & Rama Joshi. 1986. *Daughters of Independence: Gender, Caste and Class in India*. London: Zed.

Madonsela, Thuli. 2016. State of Capture. https://es.scribd.com/document/329757870/State-of-Capture-14-October-2016#download&from_embed

Naidoo, Muthal. 1997. The Search for a Cultural Identity: A Personal View of South African "Indian" Theatre. *Theatre Journal*, 49 (1) Performing (In) South Africa. March: 29-39.

Pickard-Cambridge, Claire. 1989. *The Greying of Johannesburg*. Johannesburg: SAIRR.

Robinson, Guy M & Doris A. Carson. 2016. Resilient communities: transitions, pathways and resourcefulness. *The Geographical Journal*, 182 (2) June: 114–122. https://doi.org/10.1111/geoj.12144

Rose, J. Coplen. 2015. The Limits of Unity in Ashwin Singh's *To House*: Food, South African Indian Ethnicity and Drama from Durban. In: F. Hand & E. Pujolràs-Noguer (eds). *Relations and Networks in South African Indian Writing*. Leiden: Brill Rodopi: 153-177.

Ryan, Louise. 1995. Traditions and double moral standards: the Irish suffragists' critique of nationalism. *Women's History Review*, 4:4, 487-503. https://doi.org/10.1080/09612029500200095

Sachs, Albie. 1990. *Protecting Human Rights in a New South Africa*. Cape Town: Oxford University Press.

Scott, Katy. 2019. South Africa is the world's most unequal country. 25 years of freedom have failed to bridge the divide. https://edition.cnn.com/2019/05/07/africa/south-africa-elections-inequality-intl/index.html

Shrestha, Anushiya. 2019. Which community, whose resilience? Critical reflections on community resilience in peri-urban Kathmandu Valley. *Critical Asian Studies*, 51 (4): 493-514. https://doi.org/10.1080/14672715.2019.1637270

Steadman, Ian. 1991. Theatre Beyond Apartheid. *Research in African Literatures*, 22 (3): 77-90

Suzman, Janet. 2014. Stage directions in South Africa. *Index on Censorship* 43 (2): 158-163 https://doi.org/10.1177/0306422014534578

Walker, B, L. Gunderson, A. Kinzig, C. Folke, S. Carpenter, & L. Schultz. 2006. A Handful of Heuristics and Some Propositions for Understanding Resilience in Social-ecological Systems. *Ecology and Society* 11 (1): 13. http://www.ecologyandsociety.org/vol11/iss1/art13/

Walters, Leoné, Manoel Bittencourt & Carolyn Chisadza. 2019. Public Infrastructure Provision and Ethnic Favouritism: Evidence from South Africa. Working Paper 2019-49. http://www.up.ac.za/media/shared/61/WP/wp_2019_49.zp175390.pdf

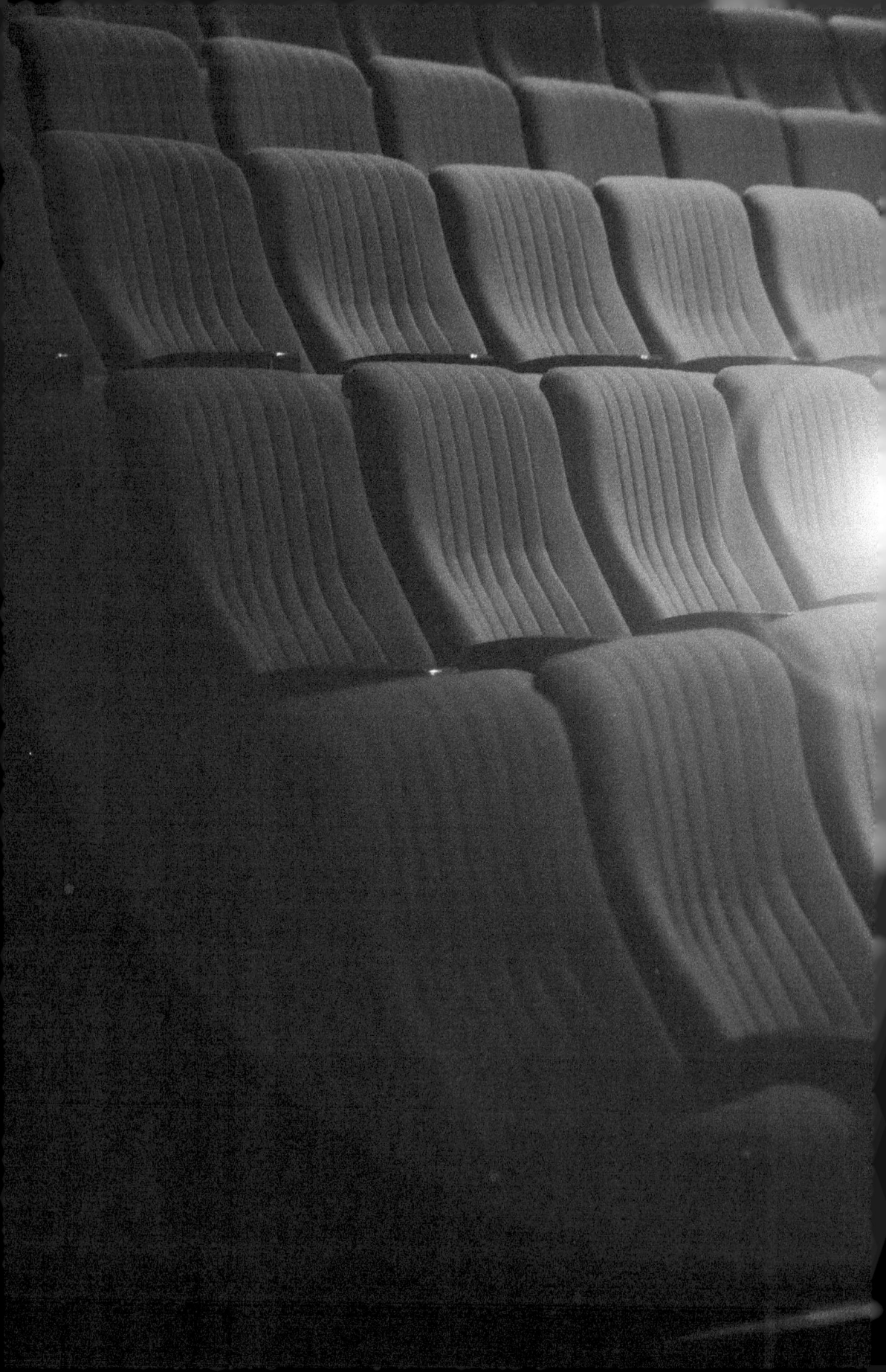

ACT 3

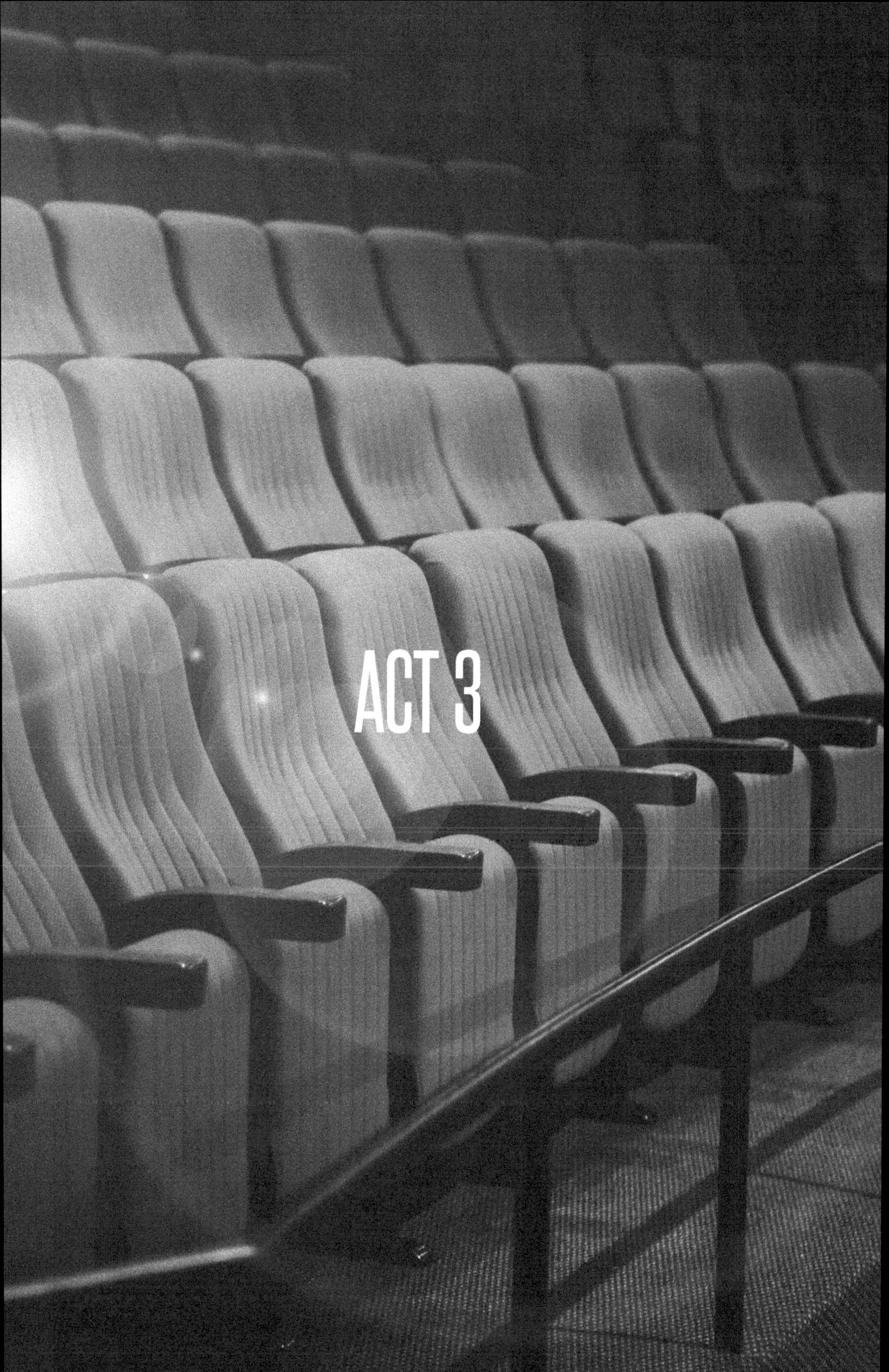

SCENE 1

A Director's Cut

Staging the Plays

Ralph Lawson

An abiding mystery, no doubt, to the average theatre goer is what, precisely, the director does. What is the nature of their contribution? How, and to what extent, do they influence a production? Their name appears in the programme and on the poster perhaps, they have their own chair in the rehearsal room sometimes, actors quail at the thought of incurring their displeasure; they are mentioned in reviews (not always, more often only when a production misses the mark) and interviews, but these seldom get beyond peripheries and the questions remain unanswered.

> Occasionally a layman will speculate wildly:
> "Do you go to every rehearsal?"
> Yes.
> "Do the actors have to do what you tell them to?"
> Definitely (though you can make them believe it was all their idea)
> "Is a director really necessary?"
> Oh, yes!
> "Why?"
> Well ...

Simon Callow, the eminent actor, director and author of the autobiographical *Being an Actor,* recalls his mother enquiring what it was that a director did once he had told the actors where to stand.

What indeed?

There is no doubt that a theatrical performance cannot be a free for all. Actors have highly developed survival instincts and will thrust themselves into the foreground at the drop of a hat, at the expense of the greater good. They're programmed to do this, after all. One might liken a band of actors to an army about to engage in conflict. No good rushing in with blood-curdling cries and guns blazing; there has to be a definite plan of action and a chain of command to set it in motion.

History tells us that there was, indeed, a time when the theatre flourished without the intervention of a director. The cut and thrust of the stage of the eighteenth and nineteenth centuries relied almost exclusively on the prowess of leading actors, many of them truly brilliant by all accounts, who made the play their own by taking the most prominent position on the stage, dead centre, declaiming the text and literally hogging the limelight (Burton, 1960; Brockett & Hildy, 2013). Coleridge described with awe the performances of Edmund Kean, the great tragedian of the Romantic period, who played Shakespeare as if to the accompaniment of flashes of lightning (Coleridge, 1823). Very impressive, no doubt, but one might conclude that all that remained of the play itself was a charred ruin. Ironically, two hundred years previously Shakespeare himself railed against such treatment of his work. Frustrated, one imagines, by the lack of a director to see to it that style in performance matched the emotional truth he was at such pains to invoke, he put into the mouth of one of his most serious-minded characters, Hamlet, a string of caveats to performers aimed at eradicating such excesses.[1] He exhorted them not to "mouth", or exaggerate, their lines, to speak them naturally, "trippingly on the tongue"; neither to "saw the air" with exaggerated gesture nor to "tear a passion to tatters"; never to overdo things, since this, he maintained, would be contrary to the "very purpose of playing" which is, was and always will be, "to hold the mirror up to nature". We realise now how spot on he was. But little changed. A couple of centuries later, David Garrick, the great actor of the eighteenth century, did make some concession by at least attempting to observe the play as a unified whole; but the Bard's advice was still routinely flouted.[2] Without the objective eye of a director, actors continued to out-Herod Herod with reckless abandon. This lasted well into the late nineteenth century, the era of the actor-manager who trotted out his most celebrated performances with little regard for the play or the efforts of his supporting company (Pearson, 1950). Audiences of the day expected it and revelled in it. Catharsis flowed on a tide of melodrama and all was well. Until the collective social conscience reared its head.

Realism in the Theatre

Charles Dickens, in his novels, had already begun to caricature the Victorian actor's excessive style with characters like Vincent Crummles (*Nicholas Nickleby*) and Mr Wopsle (*Great Expectations*); at the same time, and on a far more serious note, he drew attention to the appalling social conditions of the time, the grim facts of life in the slums and the plight of the working class, public hanging, child labour and the inequality that lay beneath the veneer of so-called civilization.

---

1   *Hamlet* Act III, Scene ii

2   G.C. Lichtenberg, a German professor from the University of Gottingen, recorded Garrick's reaction, as Hamlet, to his first encounter with the Ghost: "[He] turns suddenly about, at the same instant starting with trembling knees two or three steps backward; his hat falls off; his arms, especially the left, are extended straight out, the left hand as high as his head, the right arm is more bent, and the hand lower, the fingers are spread far apart; and the mouth open; thus he stands one foot far advanced before the other, in a graceful attitude, as if petrified". (*New Variorum* 269-70), quoted in Borlik, 2007: 5.

Soon playwrights like Ibsen had joined the fray, followed by Chekov, Shaw and others, who spear-headed the new movement towards realism in the theatre. Ibsen tackled subjects that included venereal disease (*Ghosts*) and women's rights (*A Doll's House*), forcing his audience to re-examine their moral standpoint. Shaw, too, highlighted the emancipation of women as well as class division (*Pygmalion*) and wrote plays about prostitution (*Mrs Warren's Profession*) and slum conditions (*Widowers' Houses*) while Chekhov portrayed the quavering death throes of the landed gentry in the face of the rising Russian proletariat (*The Cherry Orchard*) through the masterful expression of natural thought, speech and behaviour. Dramatists began to define the human condition as never before. There were others like the nineteenth century playwright T.W. Robertson who made valuable contributions to the Modernist movement by providing precise stage directions and insisting on physical detail in the setting and psychologically truthful acting in a well integrated mise-en-scène. The transparency of plot-driven melodrama was being replaced by detailed characterisation and convincing settings, and its predominant subjects, murder and mayhem, were abandoned in favour of those that reflected a truer reality. Enter the director.

Interestingly, the first production of Chekhov's *The Seagull* was given a chilly reception. Audiences, presumably unaccustomed to the lack of the exuberant histrionics that were part and parcel of theatrical outings at that time, were unable to tune in to the subtleties of expression, the underlying thought and emotion that defined the new subject matter (McDonald, 1993). The playwright was discouraged to the extent that he decided to give up writing for the theatre until an actor named Konstantin Stanislavski took the piece and restaged it with the concise direction needed to breathe life into it. He mined the "subtext", what was unsaid as much as what was said, encouraging the actors to study human behaviour and to draw from their own as well as imagined experience to create the characters and, above all, to find truthful psychological motivation for the dramatic interaction. His "system" of training and rehearsal practice, including innovations like improvisation and textual analysis, is still widely employed and might be considered a benchmark for directors to this day. This, then, can begin to define the director's task (Stanislavski, 1924 & 1989).

Suspending Disbelief as Never Before

It is reasonable to assume that the discomfort experienced by audiences of what had become known as the New Drama had as much to do with the challenge to their moral standpoint as it did to the manner in which the new ideas were presented. The new realism extended beyond the subject matter to, as we have seen, a fresh and more naturalistic acting style. Set and costume design, lighting and props became representations of the real thing. Everything was now geared to portray a genuine slice of life that was intended to be interchangeable with the real world, to "hold the mirror up to nature" as convincingly as possible in order to get its trenchant messages across (Styan, 1983). Theatre goers were forced to engage with what was happening on stage in an entirely new way; and in order to achieve this, playwrights and their new allies, directors, were required to suspend their audiences' disbelief as never before.

Coined by Samuel Taylor Coleridge a hundred years earlier, the phrase "suspension of disbelief" (Safire, 2007) was first proposed as a means for the reader to extract the maximum benefit from a poetical work that contained reference to, for example, the supernatural, a subject that re-appeared in the Romantic imagination in the wake of the rational thinking of the eighteenth century. It has since found an important, and possibly more useful, application in relation to the theatre. By implication, an audience is required to "buy in" to a dramatic situation wholeheartedly in order to engage successfully with it. They will be aware, naturally, that the actor playing Hamlet has not succumbed to real wounds, but that will not diminish their appreciation of the climax of that play as long as they are able to suspend their disbelief. In the prologue to *Henry V*, Shakespeare, who expressed so much that is still pertinent to dramatic art in the twenty-first century, asks his audience to engage their "imaginary forces" to create, in the confines of the Globe Theatre, the turmoil of the battle fields of France, to see the armies, horses and weaponry, to imagine the splendour of princes and kings and to travel with them through time and space. This is, of course, a direct plea to them to suspend their disbelief. Setting the scene on the eve of the great battle of Agincourt, he asks them to "entertain conjecture of a time when creeping murmur and the poring dark fills the wide vessel of the universe" (Act IV), a superbly evocative picture of night that was particularly necessary since his plays were originally performed during the day. A modern director, with the improved means at their disposal, will nevertheless work as tirelessly to assist their audience to engage their imaginary forces by avoiding, in performance or presentation, anything that doesn't emanate from a point of truth. The breath-taking technology employed in modern films has increased the onus on theatre makers to leave no stone unturned in their endeavours to convince their audiences, particularly if they wish to lure them from the dazzling effects on display in the cinema, that what is happening on stage is real. Modern techniques of screen acting, it is interesting to note, are built on Stanislavski's system, introduced to the industry as the 'Method' by Lee Strasberg, Stella Adler and Sanford Meisner in the 1950's to achieve the micro-realism that that medium demands (Krasner, 2010, 129-130). To compete in the live theatre, then, the director's prime concern must be the creation of an even greater suspension of disbelief. If that is diligently engaged throughout, the rest will follow.

If Stanislavski's insistence on truth underpins the presentation style of today, what of the myriad departures from realism that one encounters in the work of, say, Brecht, Pirandello or his successors, the Absurdists? What of plays like

Ionesco's *The Bald Prima Donna* in which a clock strikes seventeen? What of the episodic structure of plays like *Reoca Light* that defy the unities deemed necessary by Aristotle for "an imitation of action" (1907) and in which one actor inhabits the personas of a dozen or more characters? The keynote here would be the development by the director of an appropriate concept, based on the playwright's vision, with a corresponding style of presentation to support it - consistency in the latter is of particular importance - based on the inherent truth of any given situation. They can depart from the rigours of absolute naturalism and invoke the abstract to great effect as long as they remain true to life. The clock that strikes seventeen in Ionesco's play would be seen, then, not as a clown-like gimmick that provokes a low comic reaction but as something more serious, even menacing, such as one encounters beneath the superficially mundane situations in plays by Pinter. The Absurdist playwrights employed seemingly ridiculous devices to promulgate serious ideas (von Stein, 2019). A slap-stick reaction to the clock by the characters on stage would be inappropriate. A genuine reaction - it might be surprise, resignation, shock, or indifference - would be in keeping with the playwright's intention to illustrate, say, the futility of clock-watching; and as long as this reaction is true to life it will suspend disbelief in the audience and elicit an appropriate response. Farce and low comedy, in their place, rely equally upon heartfelt responses from the characters and precisely the same rules apply if genuine laughter is to be provoked. Likewise, an actor portraying a variety of characters in one play without the elaborate use of make up and costume, will be accepted readily by an audience if what motivates the characters is genuine and the style of presentation consistent.

It can be seen then that stylistic and psychological cohesion as we might call it is the most essential ingredient of a dramatic work, and a good playwright will see to it that true motivation exists for every line of dialogue and piece of action. This may not always be immediately obvious and it is the director's task to use their intuitive instincts to bring it to light. This might involve, as suggested earlier, an examination of the subtext or the use of improvisation to unlock the hidden intentions of the characters. Less obvious perhaps, but of equal importance in the pursuit of truthful representation, is correct casting and no director should underestimate the potentially negative impact that the wrong actor, irrespective of their skill, can have on a production. By the same token, a correctly cast actor can open up vistas of opportunity for interesting interpretation by virtue of the fact that they are half way there to begin with.

Acting in Ashwin Singh's Plays

For *Reoca Light* an actor of particular ability is called for, one who can portray convincingly the seventeen characters through whom the story is brought to life and, at the same time, meet the physical demands of a one-hander. A knowledge of and a familiarity with the cultural background of the play is also essential. The latter also applies to the cast of *To House*, although the characters in this instance are deliberately drawn from a cross section of contemporary South African society; their differences are the backbone of the piece, which examines their co-existence and resultant behaviour when thrust together in a housing complex. *Into the Grey* presents a different challenge. This play examines the interaction of two characters, again from different race groups and on opposite sides of a political spectrum, over an extended period of time during which the world and their fortunes shift. Their response to new circumstances and to the changes that these have brought about personally and professionally in each other provide the dramatic interaction and a fine lens through which the playwright examines the socio-political momentum of three decades. Interestingly, he suggests that the four supporting roles are played by the same actor, the device employed in *Reoca Light*.

The director, having established the playwright's intention, will set about reflecting on the characters, their physical attributes, something of their psyche, what motivates them, the obstacles they face and the tactics they employ to overcome them. They will look for the pivotal idea, the person, object, place or event on which all the characters have an opinion and how this affects their inner lives and inter-relationships. *Reoca Light* contains a strong pivotal idea, that of disrupted ritual: lives are thrown off balance by the threatened closure of Mohan's Superette, a hub of not only social but spiritual significance to the Reoca community. Similarly, conflict in *To House* is set in motion by the disruption of order in the lives of neighbours who are unable to reconcile negatively preconceived notions of one another. A clash of differing points of view focuses the central conflict in *Into the Grey* and the extended time frame leaves many issues unresolved between the two main characters giving rise to a highly charged final confrontation.

An examination of the dialogue will reveal much about the characters' personalities, not only through what they say but how they say it. The director should therefore consider carefully what vocabulary and phrases they employ, their vocal patterns, their rhythms and emphases. The dialogue in *Reoca Light* is redolent with keenly observed idiosyncrasies of speech and expression that illuminate and reveal each personality in fine detail, while in *Into the Grey*, the playwright uses monologue in a number of scenes as a means to convey the story and to portray the internal life and inter-relationship of the characters. Jason's colloquialisms and repeated expletives in *To House* tell of his inner conflict and insecurity while the placatory words and phrases given to Sanjay indicate a more passive, self-effacing personality.

Directing Ashwin Singh's Plays

Having considered the means by which the playwright has set their intention in motion, the director will begin to develop a concept to bring it to life. This will include a practical interpretation of the suggested setting, as outlined in the stage directions, in the appropriate style. The action of *Reoca Light* takes place in a disused convenience store and in a prefabricated hut behind it which, we learn, is in the process of being moved to another location. Of the three works, it is clearly the most story driven; *To House* could be seen to be more character driven, perhaps, and *Into the Grey* more circumstance driven. This will influence the director's concept in each case. Anthropologists tell us that when the language of primitive man moved beyond mating and danger calls, the constructs he developed quickly evolved into stories with which we began to create the human experience. Stories, we know, play an integral part in the development of our social and moral behaviour and we recognise them as sources of elucidation, edification or entertainment; the simple story-telling element in *Reoca Light* could thus be effectively exploited in conceptualising it for performance. This was achieved by minimising furniture, props and costume, dispensing with realistic elements in the setting and concentrating on the narrative. Single items of costume differentiated the characters, a hat for Uncle Johnny, a scarf for Mrs Singh, and props like a tea cup and a cricket bat were created through the use of mime. The physical dynamic was created by a suggestion throughout of items being packed up in the hut prior to its relocation and simple boxes were moved around at appropriate moments as the narrative unfolded. This action could then be interrupted by the re-enactment of various incidents in the story, prompted by the discovery of items that had been consigned to the boxes, for example a cricket ball and Manoj's apron. *To House* required greater examination of the inner lives of the characters and their resultant personas, and more attention to details of costume and props including consumable food and drink, as well as the creation of a more realistic, on the surface at least, environment. This had to suggest two identical town houses on the ground floor of a complex as well as a section of the garden outside and the park opposite. Appropriate furniture was required to suggest the occupants' preoccupation with image and one-upmanship. Detail in sourcing the right brand of whisky, for instance, was therefore important. The setting and visual detail in *Into the Grey* is more expressive of the external forces at play behind the narrative and consequently realistic items of furniture were dispensed with as far as possible and attention was focused on realistic props and costumes in an environment that was abstract yet flexible enough to suggest a number of locations including a university courtyard, a hospital, a community centre (later burnt out) and a street in Chatsworth.

Having outlined their concept, the director will start to devise, possibly with an appointed designer, a set for the production. This will accommodate specific outlines suggested by the playwright and include a number of practical considerations like the size of the stage on which the production is to be mounted and the resources available. At this point they will be aware of the inherent dynamics of the piece and must ensure that the space they are creating will enable the realisation of the correct dramatic momentum. They should, therefore, anticipate the movement of the actors within the set which in turn, as we have seen, will be motivated by their thought processes and personality types; a character who is inclined to be cerebral will move with a an energy that is distinct from one who operates on a more visceral level. Devising the patterns of movement about the stage is referred to as "blocking" and a large part of early rehearsal will be dedicated to creating momentum for the characters that reflects their inner experience from moment to moment and, at the same time, creates an overall dynamic that serves the play as a whole. Hiatus is the enemy of suspension of disbelief and careful blocking will ensure satisfactory and convincing dramatic flow. Upon reflection it was decided not to recreate two identical settings in mirror image for *To House* since, quite apart from economic considerations, there was the question of space; fifty percent of the acting area would be unused for half the time and the space required for the scenes that take place in the garden and in the park would have been compromised. Added to this, the picture of two separate interiors that are essentially the same was deemed less interesting than the suggestion that the lives of the inhabitants literally overlap in spite of their perceived differences. The solution was a single set that consisted of two front doors on either side of the stage, each of a different colour, with a large window between them that served either unit. Beyond this was the garden area and beyond the garden a raised area with a bench and the suggestion of trees to indicate the park. The source of light shifted from stage left to stage right depending on the unit that featured from scene to scene and subtle colour washes were employed to further differentiate the units.

The expressionistic design indicated in the stage directions for *Into the Grey* was realised by the creation of a strong presence of the red brick structures of the institutions that dominate the lives of the main characters, the university courtyard and the hospital. Different colours were used in the background lighting to suggest, in broad strokes, the often highly-charged mental states of the characters. These were played onto translucent windows to provide the necessary claustrophobic atmosphere and staircases suggested the presence of unseen, potentially sinister forces beyond them and provided the opportunity for jagged physical momentum as the characters traversed them in a desperate attempt to escape. The set was versatile and could be used effectively for interior as well as exterior scenes and it was dominated by a large window that served as a back-projection screen. Light was thrown onto the back of it which rendered the figures behind it visible in silhouette, a useful device that further emphasised the underlying menace and hinted at the techniques associated with the expressionist cinema of the early twentieth century in which realism is distorted for emotional effect. The shadow device was also extremely useful in staging effectively the murder and other acts of violence and bloodshed without recourse to the graphic detail that would have been necessary and difficult to provide convincingly in the close confines of the small theatre in which the play was presented. Gobos were used in the night scene in the burnt out youth centre to assist with the illusion of destruction; these are small slides with shapes cut into them which are placed in front of the lens of a spotlight to create a mottled effect. In this scene, Logan and Sandile used torches, which added a good deal of suspense to the dramatic interplay and suggested, at the same time, that the electricity supply had been disrupted.

It can be seen, then, that another element that is indispensable in the creation of a convincing production is stage lighting. A director will usually work with a lighting designer, or at least a skilled technician, to execute their ideas; but there is a string of rules which they must observe in the process, the most obvious being that visibility is essential at all times. Poor visibility will diminish the audience's attention very rapidly, by compromising their ability not only to see what is taking place but to hear the dialogue. Playing comedy successfully, particularly, requires good lighting, which stands to reason since a good deal of it is visual, even in verbal comedy where the reactions of the characters must be seen in order to punctuate a comic moment. A dramatic scene will be enhanced by atmospheric lighting, certainly, but the effect will be lost if the actors' expressions and their reactions are shrouded by insufficient illumination. Lighting and the effects it is intended to produce should be high on the list of the director's priorities as they consider a concept through which to breathe life into a playwright's work and will be developed in tandem with the set design. The mystical element in *Reoca Light*, the light that appears at the moment of Sunil's epiphany for example calls, obviously, for a special effect; but there are other subtleties that can enhance the narrative and keep the audience's attention focused. Colour changes are very useful and can be instigated by the flick of a switch on modern computerised equipment while changes in intensity can contribute to the shifting emotion of a scene very effectively. Sunil's spontaneous impersonations of Themba, Golden, Mr Singh or Bruno, the dog, could be literally highlighted, or not, in accordance with the situations in which these characters find themselves at a given moment. Cold colours like blue can create a tangible feeling of night or enhance a negative atmosphere and were employed in the Zakir Ally and Manoj/Mrs Singh scenes in the hut, while warmer hues like amber and gold were used to create the exterior scenes. The simple platform upon which the narrative of *Reoca Light* unfolds was achieved by defining an acting area that suggested the store with an adjacent smaller one to represent the hut. The first was created with a piece of vinyl of the kind used to clad flooring and was chosen for its pattern. The smaller area was slightly raised and a "star cloth" - a drop studded with small light bulbs to represent a night sky - was used to depict Sunil's moment of elevated consciousness. This, along with the raised platform, was dispensed with in a later production at the Tara Theatre in London when, interestingly, it was discovered that the effectiveness of the story was increased by simpler lighting and a far less cluttered approach. The opening and closing monologues, spoken by the one character that stands outside the piece, so to speak, as the ancestral presence, Areendum Mohan Rastogi, was pre-recorded using a particular acoustic. In performance, the actor playing Sunil mouthed the speech, effectively portraying his great-great-grandfather and suggesting, at the same time, the character's existence in another dimension.

The rehearsal process itself will commence with several readings of the play and an in-depth discussion of its themes, its characters, their motivations, and the envisaged concept of the production. The director will acknowledge at all times the thoughts and instincts of the cast and allow for a degree of experimentation when called for in order to arrive at a consensus. The actors, after all, will ultimately bring their concept to life and their individual sense of ownership of the work should be engendered at an early stage. To this end, they will suggest means to obtain the results they are after rather than insist on them. They will endeavour to create fertile ground for the actor's art to take root and flourish and nurture their development; they will be mindful at all times of their safety and comfort. And they will be aware constantly of that sage reminder by Rudyard Kipling that "'the strength of the pack is the wolf and the strength of the wolf is the pack" (2008: 165).

The next stage of rehearsal involves sketching an outline of the moves. These will be developed and revised as rehearsals progress and the internal lives of the characters emerge more vividly and the inherent dynamics of the play reveal themselves. At this point the director might suggest improvisation as a means to determine hidden aspects of character relationship or to tap into the essence of a dramatic situation. An imagined first meeting between Kajol and Sibusiso, say, could reveal a number of behavioural traits that are not obvious from their interaction in *To House*; an imagined encounter between Deena and Sanjay, who have little interaction in the play, could be instrumental nevertheless in bringing to light aspects of the personalities of both characters. Letter writing is a powerful improvisation exercise that can articulate a character's inner thoughts concerning a relationship or situation with surprising clarity; such expression can bring any number of subconscious thoughts to light which the actor can then add to their subtext, even if the letter is addressed to an imagined character that does not appear in the play, for example Logan's wife or Sanjay's mother. Subtext will then inform behaviour which, in turn, informs blocking. The type of prop (any practical object that is required in a scene, from a cigarette to a tea-cup or an automatic rifle) should shed light on the personality of the character that uses it, and the manner in which they do so can add a considerable dimension to an actor's performance. Sibusiso's preoccupation with the material trappings of his upwardly mobile existence, for example, was implied by his preference for fine wine. His lack of interest in Kajol's domestic problems was highlighted by his selfish behaviour in ignoring her and photographing, with an appropriate state-of-the-art cell phone, his newly-acquired recliner instead. Later, in response to a further appeal for sympathy, he is seen to focus self-indulgently on the ritual of opening a bottle of vintage wine and tasting it.

Details of costume should be carefully considered and create as vividly as possible a visual interpretation of character. This can be achieved simply, as mentioned previously with reference to *Reoca Light*, where items like hats, scarves and a pair of spectacles were added to a basic costume in a neutral colour. A more realistic look was required for the costumes in *To House* - Jason's disappointment with life in general and his alternating bouts of aggression and depression indicated a seedy attire, a dishabille consisting of a much-worn dressing gown and vest, for example; and *Into the Grey* presented the unique challenge of following the characters through several decades, from their early years as students to their middle age as successful professionals. In the first scene in which Sandile appears as a young student the actor in question was provided with a wig that was shed in the later scenes with convincing effect, while the actor portraying Logan was able to suggest successfully the changes wrought upon the characters by the passage of time simply by an increased gravitas of delivery and behaviour as the play progressed.

Naturally, every director will see things differently and there can be no definitive handbook on their craft. Interpretation is, after all, nothing more than stylistic representation or the assignment of meaning and as such is entirely subjective. It should be remembered, however, that their work is always the result of extensive collaboration. First, with the playwright, then with the actors, the designers, the technicians and the producers, who will all make a personal contribution to the final product. A good director will value these contributions, embrace them and learn from them. For the edifices they create will dissolve like sculptures built in sand and they will constantly be called upon to re-invent themselves.

Bibliography

Aristotle. 1907. *The Poetics of Aristotle*. (Samuel Henry Butcher, transl.). (4th ed.) London: Macmillan.

Borlik, Todd Andrew. 2007. 'Painting of a sorrow': Visual Culture and the Performance of Stasis in David Garrick's *Hamlet*, *Shakespeare Bulletin*, Vol 25 (1): 3-31.

Brockett, Oscar G. & Hildy, Franklin J.. 2013. *History of the Theatre*. London: Pearson Education Ltd.

Burton, E. J. 1960. *The British Theatre 1100-1900*. London: Herbert Jenkins.

Coleridge, Samuel Taylor, *Table Talk*, 27 April 1823. http://www.gutenberg.org/cache/epub/8489/pg8489-images.html

Kipling, Rudyard. 2008 [1894] *The Jungle Book*, W.W. Robson (ed) Oxford: World's Classics.

Krasner, David (2010) Strasberg, Adler and Meisner: Method Acting. In: A. Hodge (ed), *Actor Training*, London: Routledge. 144-163.

McDonald, Jan. 1993. Chekhov, Naturalism and the Drama of Dissent: Productions of Chekhov's Plays in Britain before 1914. In: P. Miles (ed). *Chekhov on the British stage*. New York: Cambridge UP: 29-42.

Pearson, Hesketh. 1950. *The Last Actor-Managers (Sir Herbert Tree)*, London: Methuen & Co. Ltd.

Stanislavski, Konstantin. 1924. *My Life in Art*, (J.J. Robbins, transl.). New York: Little Brown & Company.

Stanislavski, Konstantin, 1989 [1936]. *An Actor Prepares*, (Elizabeth Reynolds Hapgood, transl.). New York: Routledge.

Styan, J.L. 1983. *Modern Drama in Theory and Practice. Vol 1: Realism and Naturalism*. Cambridge: Cambridge UP.

Safire, William. On Language; Suspension of Disbelief. *New York Times*. 7 October 2007.

von Stein, Juana Cristina. 2019. The Theater of the Absurd and the Absurdity of Theater: The Early Plays of Beckett and Ionesco. In: E. Penskaya, Elena & J. Küpper, Joachim. *Theatre as Metaphor*, Berlin: De Gruyter. 217-237. https://doi.org/10.1515/9783110622034

SCENE 2

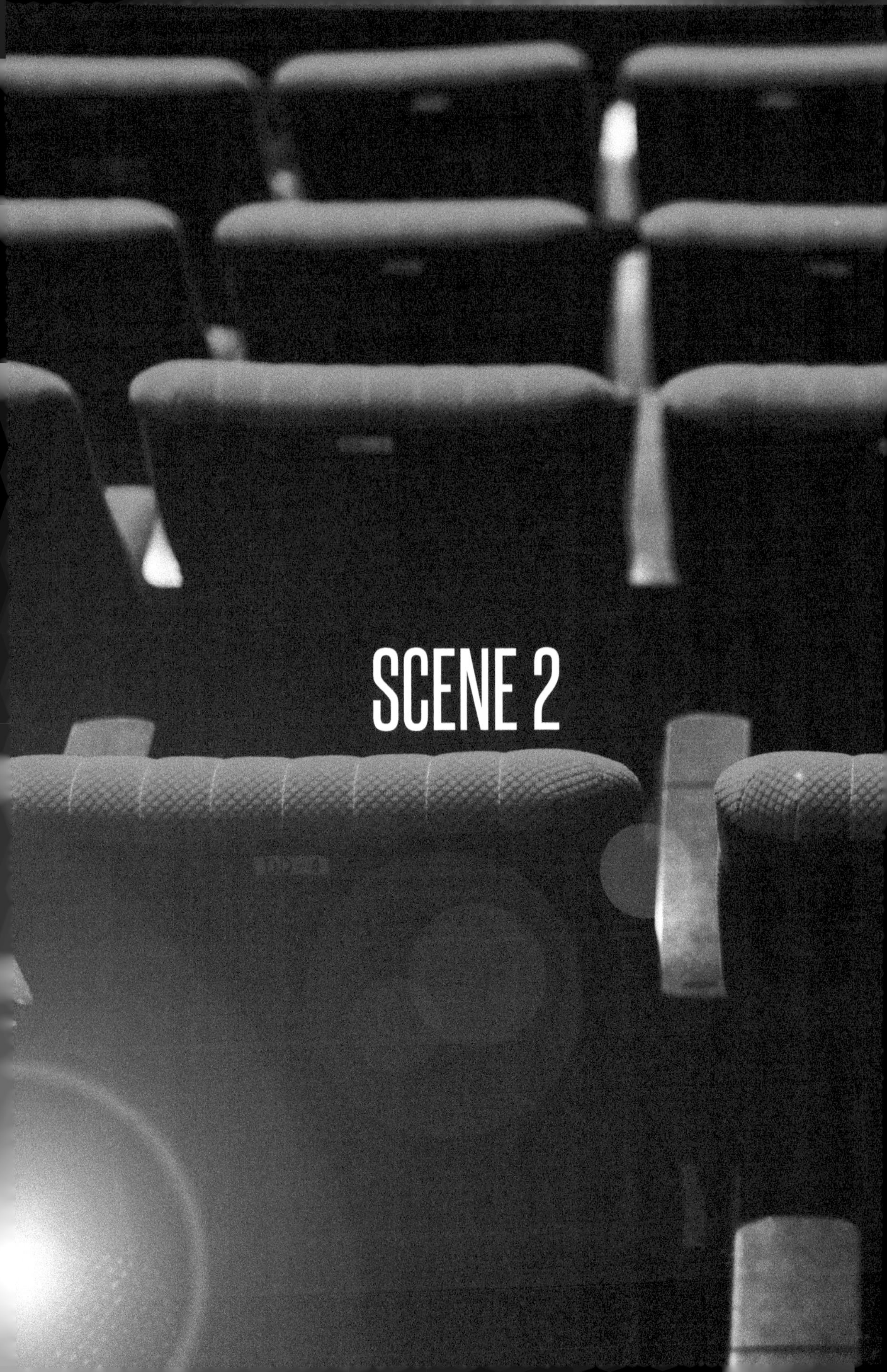

How to Swing the Game of Life in South Africa

Pallavi Rastogi

I first met Ashwin Singh in 2005 when I visited South Africa to interview the fiction writers I discuss in my book, *Afrindian Fictions: Diaspora, Race, and National Desire in South Africa* (2008). Indian South African writing was a relatively unrecognized body of work then. But it was well on its way to make its mark as a distinct field of writing with its own thematic concerns and formal conventions. At that point, fiction dominated Indian South African literature. Yet, at least one fiction-writer, who had turned his hand at drama, also towered over the world of Indian South African literature. Ronnie Govender shot to prominence with his play, *The Lahnee's Pleasure* (1980), which articulated many of the themes associated with Indian South African writing: the century-long displacement of the community through indenture, Indians as the "middle men" or the buffer zone between black and white South Africans, the blank space that was "Indianness," still needing to be filled with a self-recorded history, the fraught allegiances with other non-white communities in the apartheid and post-apartheid era, and, above all, the hard-won *full* participatory citizenship for Indians in South Africa.

I interviewed Govender, Ahmed Essop, Aziz Hassim, Deena Padayachee, and Praba Moodley for my book. Writers of immense talent and tremendous courage, their work was infused with a political agenda—a term I do not use pejoratively here—to assert national belonging in South Africa and to show the community's long participation in the Struggle for freedom. After talking to these authors, and, of course, reading their work carefully, I could already tell that my book was making a predetermined argument about the themes prevalent in the Indian South African writing coming of age in the early twenty-first century. While Ashwin's plays were also a template for mapping the key themes of Indian South African literature, the genre of drama, as well as his own unique creative sensibility, opened a new window of understanding into Indian South African culture.

I interacted with Ashwin in Durban at length in 2005. I knew he wrote plays and performed stand-up comedy. I had never read his work till he sent me his earliest plays, *Duped* and *To House*. As someone inherently partial to fiction, I have never enjoyed reading plays as much as I enjoyed reading Ashwin's work. The futuristic sci-fi setting of *Duped*, telescoping into outer space and simultaneously microscoping into crucial questions about Indians in South Africa, was formal innovation not seen often in Indian South African literature. Most of the work I was reading and writing about was set in the post-apartheid present of the new South Africa or restlessly returned to the indentured or passenger routes of migration to retrace the foundational fateful journeys that led Indians to the continent, such as Imraan Coovadia's *The Wedding* (2001) and Praba Moodley's *The Heart Knows No Colour* (2004). Even dramatist Rajesh Gopie's *Coolie Odyssey* (2002) used theatre as a platform to understand the history of Indian arrival in South Africa. *Duped*, however, evoked the past, present, and the future of South Africa, mocked the false solidarity in the new South Africa, even creating characters with chips of manufactured racial tolerance inserted in them. And in the background, the ANC government, with its celestial rhetoric of the Rainbow Nation, mercilessly reinforced the divisions that apartheid perpetrated, concealing the menace of racial division under the "still different but one nation" discourse of Rainbowism. As sociologist Ashwin Desai says, "the emergence of the 'Rainbow Nation' signalled for many the beginning of new things. However, under the rubric of the rainbow it became apparent that the past was imposing itself on the present. For those who envisaged the loosening of their ethnic clothing they soon found it sticking more closely to their bodies as the political settlement unfolded" (in Rastogi, 2008: 15). Both *Duped* and *To House*, either directly or obliquely, critique the reinforcement of ethnic identity, aligning their themes closely to other Indian South African writing, even as the plays themselves enacted formal departures from the creative conventions of the time.

I lost touch with Ashwin in the next few years but when we established contact again, it came as no surprise that his career as a playwright, as a brave new voice in South African theatre, that went *Beyond the Big Bangs*—readers familiar with Ashwin's work will recognize the reference to the title of one of his plays—to a really explosive launch on the South African stage. Ashwin was writing prolifically, publishing widely, and his plays were being performed across the world. I was able to catch up with most of his other work and see for myself how the raw talent displayed in his earlier work had matured into a nuanced literary voice that was still characterized by his hallmark crackling prose and witty, even wicked, humour. Ashwin continued to be interested in the political life of his country and his community though. The end of apartheid led to an inevitable disillusionment with the new political dispensation, which was reflected in the cultural products of the new nation, including Indian South African literature. Yet, formal literary experimentation blossomed into infinite variety. Ashwin had demonstrated an interest in experimenting with literary form even earlier with *Duped*, abandoning the heavy realism or historical return that characterized most of Indian South African literature at the turn of the century. He was always already ahead of his time.

Ashwin is also essentially a Durban writer. The city infuses his words, the ways his characters interact with each other, the emotional intensity they display, and the language they use. Durban infuses Ashwin's work with its specific complexities.

Yet, Ashwin is <u>not</u> a local writer: he is a generous and expansive humanist whose plays speak to everyone.

Focus on Swing

The rest of this Afterword focuses on *Swing* (2015) to show how a play that still maintains an interest in the themes characterizing Indian South African literature in the early twenty-first century is also preoccupied with the new themes concerning the Indian community a decade later, at a crucial time for diasporics and immigrants all over the world. As Shantal Singh states in her introductory preface to *Durban Dialogues: Then and Now*, "despite a progressive constitution South Africa remains a society divided on race, culture, and class issues" (2017: 14). *Swing* stages these divisions of race, culture, and class to consider some of the most difficult questions about South African identity today.

The stage directions of *Swing* are simple. Two long lines are cut across the stage, representing the tram line and the service line of a tennis court. The stark backdrop is elaborated with a painting or a projection of Samantha, the lead actress, rocking on a swing with Ram, her father; another projection shows her in "warrior mode on the tennis court" (Sw 101). Two actors play the roles of Samantha and her father, who is her tennis coach, as well as the other characters in the play. Samantha is not just seeking glory in the tennis court for herself. She is also playing for her father, who has transferred his hopes of sporting success on to her, and the Indian community. In this sense, Samantha shows how the success of the individual members of a marginalized community honours—or shames—that community itself.

Yet, Samantha also represents the new generation of all South Africans, born in the post- apartheid period, where life, and its amenities, come easy. Even though Samantha's father, Ram, constantly tells her stories of the daily privations and humiliations under apartheid, his tortured tales do not have much of an impact on his daughter. The first scene thus swings between Samantha's prowess at tennis and her father's dreams and aspirations for a truly free South Africa where race will no longer hold talent back. To be allowed to date Nikita, Samantha's "coloured mother", Ram had to swing his cricket bat to win a game against Nikita's family. True to its title, the play swings between past memories and present events, pessimism and optimism, the cricket bat and the tennis racket.

Swing also enacts the conflict between the coloured and the Indian communities who are unable to transcend their differences, despite occupying the middle role on the black and white spectrum of race relations in South Africa. The body of the coloured-Indian child, here Samantha, becomes the battleground on which this conflict is fought. *Swing* reflects on how the friction between demographically minor communities such as Indians and Coloureds interfere with the coalition-building that could bestow both groups with more political and cultural power. Cricket and tennis are metaphors here. The game the characters play is the game of life.

Racial difference, therefore, enters the game of life too, even in the new South Africa. Samantha's mother takes a nursing offer in Dubai, telling her:

> I am not going to move forward here…You know they call us black when it suits their agenda…then we're Indian and Coloured when that agenda suddenly changes…and on it goes like that. You won't understand now. Hopefully you won't have to experience that…although I doubt our young leaders will turn out very different. (Sw 117)

In *Afrindian Fictions*, I had observed that non-black authors asserted their place in South Africa under the new dispensation even as they critiqued the post-apartheid government for failing to nurture the most minor of its minorities: Ahmed Essop's *The Third Prophecy* (2004), which derides the new government for its inability to provide safe harbour to Muslims, is an early example of Indian disaffection in the Rainbow Nation. Yet, *Swing* refuses to give in to the despair of national failure. The play balances a mordant critique of the racial politics of post-apartheid South Africa with a robust optimism for its future.

The very title of the play opens a window into the lives of the characters. Ram relentlessly pushes Samantha into training as a tennis champion. This will sound familiar to every Indian, whose upwardly aspirational parents forced tutors in biology, science, and maths upon them to live the professionally respectable lives their parents wanted to lead. Yet, Ram wants nothing more for his daughter than to be the face of tennis in South Africa, rather than a doctor, nurse, lawyer, or engineer: those professions that Indian parents think are dedicated to their children. *Swing* beautifully complicates how parental ambitions change over time in *what* Indian parents want for their children but not *how* they want what they want for their children.

Samantha's and Ram's aspirations for tennis supremacy are torn asunder with the ascendancy of her rival, an underprivileged young black woman. As Samantha tells the journalist interviewing her,

> As my story was unfolding, there was another, much bigger event happening. I was scaling the KZN hilltops…but Lerato Sibisi, the pride of Kwamashu, was soaring above the Himalayas … She switched so easily between English and isiZulu…she seemed so simple and passionate about sport and her country…it felt like she was the epitome of the Rainbow Nation. (Sw 122-123)

If South Africa is seeking a national symbol for tennis, it has been found in Lerato Sibisi. *Swing* leaves it to the viewer/reader to conclude whether Samantha loses a championship game to Lerato because her tennis is not good enough. Or, if she succumbs to a cultural defeat in her realization that a player who is half-Indian and half-coloured, and also coached by an Indian father, can never represent the "Rainbowism" of the Rainbow Nation. The reference to the Himalayas, an Indian mountain-range, however, confuses the divisions between Samantha and Lerato, showing how Indian South Africans can climb the mountains of KZN just as black South Africans can conquer the Himalayas. South Africans are so intertwined that even the geography of their place of origin is open to the Other. *Swing* uses sport, especially the historical whiteness of tennis, to make a political point about how non-white communities fight with each other to obtain accomplishment in terms of the white world and to step into the places vacated by white champions. The play also challenges stereotypes about the academically accomplished Asian minority, focusing instead on the dreams and aspirations of a young Indian girl to become the Miss Rainbow Nation of the tennis world.

Yet, Samantha's inability, psychological or otherwise, also has a pre-history that the play interrogates in collective terms, not only through Samantha and her father but also through the successes and failures of the Indian community in South Africa. In his cricketing days, Ram is challenged to a match by his white supervisor, Rob van Vuuren with these taunting words: "You think you are something special, coolie. You think you have got the gift? You hitting a white bowler? If I used a cricket ball and really turned it on, you'd be dead (Sw 127). In a racially hierarchical society, even white people often discriminated against other white people. Ram realizes van Vuuren's fury is that of an Afrikaner who is unlikely to be selected to play for an all British county team (Sw 128). In going back in time to the apartheid-period, *Swing* connects Samantha's inability to become the Miss Rainbow Nation of the tennis world, Ram's thwarted career as an Indian cricketer during apartheid-era South Africa, and van Vuuren's frustration as an Afrikaner never selected to play for Natal. While race is certainly not a game, a game is race in this play.

The play's turn to the past also shows the collective solidarity between non-whites during the apartheid period. Ram notices that "some of my black and Indian colleagues were looking at me eagerly—they wanted me to do this for them too [defeat van Vuuren at cricket]" (Sw 128). After Ram stands his ground on the cricket field, both literally and metaphorically, Van Vuuren arrives at his bar and tells Ram that he was

> lucky. He said I'd never make it playing competitively. Week-in and week-out with real cricketers. I mean, I know that he was saying those things coz I'd hurt his pride...and a part of me wanted to beat up his arse...*I felt like I was beating up his apartheid* (Sw 129, emphasis added)

Ram transfers his rage over apartheid into his ambition for his daughter in tennis: if he cannot beat apartheid, he can at least beat its legacy of racial thinking that still prevails in the post-apartheid era.

Even though the past infringes heavily on the present, Samantha represents the future: a new horizon not only based on the Truth and Reconciliation Commission (TRC) model of forgiveness but also on a recognition that systems with majoritarian rule rarely allow minorities to excel outside of their comfort zones. This is especially true of Indians in South Africa, and elsewhere in the Indian diaspora, where young Indian people are pressured into safe, well-paying careers, and where personal happiness in professional life rarely matters. Samantha is still inspired by her father's courage to play against his nemesis in a big match: "to do that in the terrible time of our history…I was proud of him. And I knew that I had to be brave now. And to believe in myself" (Sw 130).

Since this is an Ashwin Singh play, readers should not expect the next scene to switch to Samantha winning all her serves, lobbying each ball back to her opponent no matter how out of reach it is, and defeating Lerato in straight sets. Singh is a cynic but never a despairing one: his writing always contains slivers of possibility that thrill, encourage, and uplift. Samantha loses to Lerato outright and when her father encourages her to continue playing, she firmly refuses, saying she needs time to reflect on her future.

The next scene opens with Samantha once again playing her arch-rival who is attending the University of California, Berkeley on a full scholarship. Samantha has enrolled herself in the local university and is immersed in studying to become a clinical psychologist. The evening before their match, the two women meet in the locker rooms where Lerato has stormed in after a tantrum at her coach. Samantha holds Lerato and listens to her, all the while thinking: "I thought in a less viciously competitive world…a world where performance identities were less significant…we might have been like sisters…and she agreed" (Sw 133). The two women embark on a night out on the town where Samantha eats and drinks recklessly. The gastronomical revelry, which no athlete in their right mind would partake on the eve of a crucial match, is aided and abetted by Lerato. She speaks to Samantha in honeyed tones that could come straight out of the speeches in the early days of Independence when the whole nation was drunk on the false promises of the Rainbow Nation and of Independence:

> But win or lose, we must stand together as sisters…as women…black women representing all the hopes of our generation who just want to do something meaningful with their lives. We must hold the trophy aloft together and say, 'Let's play together South Africa. It doesn't matter who wins or loses. Let's be a united nation…a proud nation. (Sw 134)

At first, Samantha is inclined to ascribe the cause of her increasing physical unease at Lerato whose persuasive powers she describes as "utterly intoxicating" (Sw 134). Once she realizes that Lerato could have been "tampering with her food"(Sw 136), she is filled with the same rebellious rage that caused her father to nearly punch van Vuuren. But, again, this is an Ashwin Singh play. The only punches that are thrown are verbal. Samantha merely contemplates violence; she never commits violence, following which Lerato pulverizes her, yet again, in the South African Open match.

Samantha's father is aghast not only at the way that Lerato sabotages Samantha's chances to win the game but also at the way the media builds up Lerato as the singular icon of South African women's tennis:

> And I kept hearing that biased commentator praising Lerato. She was the first Black tennis player to do this…and the first black athlete to do that…and I thought the moron is unaware that by so over- emphasizing her race he is doing her a disservice. But then I thought he was not even acknowledging Samantha Gopal-Johnson in any way…is she not black also…has she not achieved despite growing up in a poor neighbourhood…Is she not from a previously disadvantaged community…Is there a hierarchy of Blackness? And I saw her stumble. And I thought you cheating bastards. You took away her chance to compete. You removed fairness from the equation. (Sw 137)

If Samantha's father was only criticizing Lerato, it would be easy to see him as complicit, as were many Indians, in perpetuating the racist discourse of black people winning undeserved accomplishments in the new South Africa. Ram is railing against the *commentator*, and not against Lerato, against the system and not the individual. The commentator represents South African sporting, public, and political culture Instead of disputing Lerato's talent, Ram questions gradations of oppression instead. Why are some people less "Black" than others? How much does economic destitution matter when compared to race, especially in post-apartheid South Africa? Juxtaposing the match between Samantha and Lerato with Ram's "friendly" cricket playoff with van Vuuren further complicates a simplistic analysis of Indian racism towards what they see as undeserved black success. van Vuuren claims that Ram will never be able to enter the big league, with the white English players. Himself an Afrikaner, excluded even on the basis of language, van Vuuren too never made it into the tea-drinking, back-slapping, "good shot, I say, old chap" culture that characterized white cricket culture. In pairing Samantha and Lerato with Ram and van Vuuren, *Swing* presents sports as an allegory of nation: both apartheid and post-apartheid era South Africa sought to define who can symbolize the country by keeping its Others out.

Ram finally persuades his daughter to participate in a rematch with Lerato. Not because he wants her to become the female face of South African tennis but because he wants her to play against her most formidable opponent on equal terms:

> I just want an equal bounce…I can still feel the aura…you came to this earth to do something special. I can feel it as strongly as ever. Maybe it will be in the tennis field. Maybe as a psychologist…or perhaps as a humanitarian. But I feel that the decisive moments are getting closer and a new cycle is about to begin.

So tomorrow…just go out there and give it your best shot. And we'll applaud you. (Sw 138)

All Ram longs for is an equal bounce, on a cricket pitch or in a tennis court, where players are players and not symbols or allegories of their race. More importantly, he realizes that he cannot push his daughter into pursuing the dreams he failed to achieve. He knows she has a special purpose in the world, which she will fulfil on court or off court. As a parent, he is able to finally launch his child into the universe of self-realization *on her own terms*. Even more significantly, Samantha has graduated magna cum laude with a Masters in Psychology by this time in the play. The choice of subject is not accidental here. Psychology prepares her to understand a world in which she may not always win and also to understand that loss is not always defeat.

Samantha, thus, acquires the wisdom of her father well before he does: "I've often wondered if Lerato is obsessed with winning…pursuing the American dream rather than be guided by African ideals…But I know that the only reason I should get onto court is for the love of tennis" (138). She then recites her mother's words to Ram: "Forget who you are playing. Go back to that swing…and sway again… play without fear…and without doubt. Be free. And when you see the ball…just swing" (138). These words release Samantha from the captivity in which winning has held her for so long. The play ends with a tantalizingly incomplete match between Samantha and Lerato. Ram's fantasies may come true here. Samantha has won five straight games and is about to serve for point, game, and set (Sw 139):

> *Samantha serves powerfully and receives a soft return*
>
> Voice-over: "Oh. That one has sat up nicely for her. Will she take a swing at it"?
>
> Samantha Swings Beautifully…

If this was a generic feel-good play, Samantha would win decisively, her success displayed prominently on stage and page. In an Ashwin Singh play, the ending is more ambiguous, still subtly tracing tensions between Indian and Black South Africans even as Samantha acquires peace with winning or losing. The *in-media-res* ending opens spaces for other interpretations on the ending of the play. Instead of describing Samantha's game as inspirational, the voice-over (again, the representative of the national collective) merely claims that she is putting up "quite a fight" against a "slightly below par" Lerato (Sw 139). The voice-over refuses to assign Samantha superior skill, even if only in this particular match, and suggests instead that Lerato is the better player who is simply playing a little worse than her opponent. *Swing* does not reveal how the game will turn out. Lerato may well make a comeback. But the play is an exhortation to swing at every curveball, sending it across the net-like obstacles that are part of Indian life in South Africa. *Swing* shows the diversity of form and theme in Ashwin Singh's work even as the crucial issues it raises about Indian identity in South Africa form a continuous chain with the rest of his oeuvre.

Bibliography

Coovadia, Imraan. 2001. *The Wedding*. New York: Picador.

Gopie, Rajesh. 2002. *Coolie Odyssey*. Unpublished play, first performed 2002.

Govender, Ronnie. 1980. *The Lahnee's Pleasure*, Johannesburg: Ravan Press. Republished 2008. Johannesburg: Jacana.

Moodley, Praba. 2004. *The Heart Knows No Colour*. Cape Town: Kwela Books.

Rastogi, Pallavi. 2008. *Afrindian Fictions: Diaspora, Race, and National Desire in South Africa*. Columbus: Ohio State University Press.

Singh, Ashwin. 2017. *Durban Dialogues Then and Now*. Twickenham, UK: Aurora Metro Books.

List of Contributors

DEVARAKSHANAM (BETTY) GOVINDEN is a literary and educational scholar and poet. She is the author of the award-winning book, *Sister Outsiders – Representations of Identity and Difference in Selected Writings by South African Indian Women [2008], A Time of Memory – Reflections on Recent South African Writings [2008], and Words on Water – Reflections on Selected Writers* [2010].
herbyg@telkomsa.net

FELICITY HAND is senior lecturer in the English Department of the Autonomous University of Barcelona. She teaches post-colonial literature and history and culture of Britain and the U.S. She has published articles on various Indian Ocean writers including M.G.Vassanji, Abdulrazak Gurnah, Yasmin Alibhai-Brown and Lindsey Collen. She is the head of the research group Ratnakara http:// grupsderecerca.uab.cat/ratnakara which explores the literatures and cultures of the South West Indian Ocean. Felicity is also the editor of the electronic journal *Indi@logs. Spanish Journal of India Studies* http://revistes.uab.cat/indialogs
felicity.hand@uab.cat
https://orcid.org/0000-0002-3766-6266

PRANAV JOSHIPURA is an academic, researcher and translator. His doctoral research is on Indian playwright Mahesh Dattani. His book *A Critical Study of Mahesh Dattani's Plays* was published in 2010. Thereafter, his research has been on diaspora Indian theatre, specifically on Indian South African drama. He has translated Indian South African playwright Ashwin Singh's play *Reoca Light* into Gujarati as *Reoca no Surya* (2018). He has contributed many articles and research papers on Indian as well as Indian South African drama. Moreover, he has edited a book, *Silver Glimpses from Shabdashrusti· Selections form Modern Gujarati Prose* (2013), which is a translation of modern Gujarati prose and poetry. He has supervised several doctoral students. The author has taught English literature since 1994 at Uma Arts & Nathiba Commerce Mahila College at Gandhinagar, Gujarat, India.
pranavjoshipura@hotmail.com

RALPH LAWSON is an award-winning South African actor and director as well as an academic. He has also worked successfully in theatre in the UK and has extensive experience on radio. Lawson has been the standing director for the Playhouse Company's in-house productions and one of its chief mentors over the last decade. He has led the Company's Development Programmes, The Actor's Studio and The Community Arts Mentorship Programme for several years. His seminal drama *A Voice I Cannot Silence*, a tribute to the works of the iconic Alan Paton won several national theatre awards in 2016. Lawson has directed three of Singh's works to widespread critical acclaim, namely *Reoca Light*, To House and *Into the Grey*.
rtlawson@mweb.co.za

DEBORAH ARLENE LUTGE, a seasoned academic of over thirty years, remains an Associate Professor and HoD of the DUT Department of Drama & Production Studies, where her leadership has been acknowledged by press as forward thinking and visionary. Lutge, a Twist Theater Development Board Member, is the CCIFSA elected KZN Councilor for Arts Education and Training, as well as RITE Studios Board Member. Lutge served as regional theatre judge of professional theatre from 2001 to 2018. Saluted by her students after 25 years of service, her pedagogy received accolades from VASTA. Lutge, primarily an award winning performer and director, is in addition, a professional acting coach, a published academic, poet, and playwright; as well as a former dancer, stage combat director and choreographer.
debbiel@dut.ac.za
https://orcid.org/0000-0002-8157-6532

PALLAVI RASTOGI is Associate Professor of English at Louisiana State University in Baton Rouge, Louisiana (US). She has published widely on South Asian and South African literature, including a book, *Afrindian Fictions: Diaspora, Race and National Desire in South Africa* and an edited anthology, *Before Windrush: Recovering an Asian and Black Heritage Within Britain*. Her second book, *Postcolonial Disaster: Narrating Catastrophe in the Twenty-First Century*, was published by Northwestern University Press in April 2020. She is Associate Editor for the *South Asian Review* and also serves as Reviews Editor for the journal. She is Vice-President of the South Asian Literary Association (SALA) and board member of the American Comparative Literature Association (ACLA).
prastogi@lsu.edu
https://orcid.org/0000-0002-4010-7342

J. COPLEN ROSE is an Assistant Professor in the Department of English and Theatre at Acadia University, located in Nova Scotia, Canada. He teaches courses in fantasy fiction and postcolonial theory. Coplen completed his Ph.D. in English and Film Studies at Wilfrid Laurier University and holds a Master of Arts from Lakehead University and a Bachelor of Arts from Bishop's University. He is also currently serving as the Atlantic Representative on the Executive Council of the Canadian Association for Commonwealth Literature and Language Studies.
jcoplenrose@gmail.com
https://orcid.org/0000-0001-9474-8092

SHANTAL SINGH is a clinical psychologist and academic as well as a theatre and film producer. She has been departmental head at a tertiary-level hospital in South Africa and is currently in private practice. She has lectured psychology at both undergraduate and postgraduate levels and also has extensive supervisory experience. Singh has a particular affinity with children and in this regard has published a booklet on the dynamic interplay between parents and infants. She has also co-written a radio drama series entitled *GrandAsia Lodge*, which was broadcast on Lotus FM. Singh is the producer in the arts association *The Singh Siblings and* has been programme director at Ashwin Singh's book launches at home and abroad as well as at the 3-D Conference held in Durban in 2016. *shantalsingh211@gmail.com*

www.ingramcontent.com/pod-product-compliance
Lightning Source LLC
Chambersburg PA
CBHW052342100426
42736CB00047B/3406